Teaching Without Nonsense:
Translating Research into Effective Practice, 2nd ed.

Bertie Kingore
AUTHOR

Jeffery Kingore
GRAPHIC DESIGN

PROFESSIONAL ASSOCIATES PUBLISHING
www.kingore.com

Current Publications by
Bertie Kingore, Ph.D.

> VISIT DR. KINGORE ONLINE!
> **www.BertieKingore.com**

Alphabetters: Thinking Adventures with the Alphabet (Task cards)
Assessment: Time Saving Procedures for Busy Teachers, 4th ed.
–*Assessment Interactive CD-ROM*
Centers in Minutes!
–*Centers CD-ROM Vol. 1: Grades K-8*
–*Centers CD-ROM Vol. 2: Literacy Stations, Grades K-4*
Developing Portfolios for Authentic Assessment, PreK-3: Guiding Potential in Young Learners
Differentiation: Simplified, Realistic, and Effective
–*DIfferentiation Interactive CD-ROM*
Engaging Creative Thinking: Activities to Integrate Creative Problem Solving
Integrating Thinking: Strategies that Work! 2nd ed.
Just What I Need! Learning Experiences to Use on Multiple Days in Multiple Ways
Kingore Observation Inventory, 2nd ed.
Literature Celebrations: Catalysts for High-Level Book Responses, 2nd ed.
Reading Strategies for Advanced Primary Readers
Reading Strategies for Advanced Primary Readers: Professional Development Guide
Reaching All Learners: Making Differentiation Work!
Recognizing Gifted Potential: Planned Experiences with the KOI
We Care: A Curriculum for Preschool Through Kindergarten, 2nd ed.

FOR INFORMATION OR ORDERS CONTACT:
PROFESSIONAL ASSOCIATES PUBLISHING
PO Box 28056
Austin, Texas 78755-8056
Toll free phone/fax: 866-335-1460

> VISIT US ONLINE!
> **www.kingore.com**

Teaching Without Nonsense:
Translating Research into Effective Practice, 2nd ed.

Copyright © 2008 Bertie Kingore

Published by **PROFESSIONAL ASSOCIATES PUBLISHING**

Printed in the United States of America
ISBN: 0-9787042-5-8
ISBN: 978-0-9787042-5-4

All rights reserved. The purchase of this book entitles the individual teacher to reproduce the forms for use in the classroom. No additional reproduction, transmission, or recording of this work is permitted without the written consent of the publisher.

Bertie Kingore, Ph.D.

is an international consultant and the author of twenty-four professional books, eight interactive CD-ROMs, numerous articles, and instructional aids. She has received many honors, including the Legacy Award for the Educator Book of the Year, the first Texas Gifted Educator of the Year, and the Outstanding Alumnus Award from the University of North Texas. She also served as President of the Texas Association for the Gifted and Talented.

Dr. Kingore works with teachers and models instruction in classrooms all over the globe. She is recognized for her ability to seamlessly weave research into practice as well as her practical and humorous presentations. Her work responds to the diversity of children, encourages high-level responses and achievement, and minimizes the preparation time of educators in schools and universities.

She currently resides in Austin with her husband, Richard. For more information, please visit her website.

http://www.bertiekingore.com

Jeffery Kingore

has a B.A. in English from the University of North Texas and designed sixteen publications for state departments and national publishers. He has produced eight interactive CD-ROMs and designed websites for international companies and consultants. For more information, please visit his website.

http://www.geekgraphics.com

TRANSLATORS:

Patry Lerwick, M.Ed.
is a teacher at Plano School District and was a demonstration teacher for Dr. Sandra Kaplan. She may be reached at: lerwick2@aol.com

Tracy Spies
is a teacher at Aldine School District.

Myrna Bailey
is a teacher at Aldine School District.

Contents

Introduction — 1

Section 1: Effective, Efficient Instruction for High Achievement — 3
    Translating Research into Effective Practice — 3
    Classroom Management Without Nonsense — 6
    Open-Ended Tasks for Multiple Learning Applications — 9
    Grading Open-Ended Responses — 10
    Quick Assessment Techniques: When You Only Have a Minute — 16

Section 2: Learning Experiences — 21
    Guidelines for Success — 21
    Acrostic — 23
    Analysis Grid — 31
    Body Rhyme — 39
    Comic Character — 45
    Concept Map — 52
    Fact Puzzle — 75
    I Am — 82
    Important Thing — 94
    Scavenger Hunt — 105
    Thinking Triangle — 112
    Two-Column Chart — 125

References — 130

Introduction

In educational settings today, it is nonsense to allow:
- Instructional decisions devoid of a research base to guide practice.
- Learning experiences that are fun but do not have productive applications of concepts and skills.
- Overwhelmed educators.
- Excessive preparation and paper management for teachers, leaving less energy and enthusiasm for teaching.
- A seemingly endless supply of skill sheets requiring simple, correct answers instead of thoughtful responses that require mental engagement, process engagement, and social-emotional connections.
- A predominance of beginning-thinking tasks when high-level thinking is needed by every student and results in higher achievement.
- Passive listeners instead of active learners and responsible participants.
- Bored students!
- Bored teachers!

Teaching Without Nonsense: Translating Research into Effective Practice, 2nd ed. is a collection of research-based, simple-to-prepare learning experiences proven beneficial in thousands of classrooms. During the development, expansion, and modeling of these activities with primary through secondary students, teachers commented on the tasks' simplicity and effectiveness as they successfully applied and extended a myriad of skills and concepts in multiple content areas and topics.

Significant changes in this second edition respond to the need to integrate learning standards with increased depth and complexity. Section One is largely new content that details:
- The research base for the inclusion of these practices,
- Classroom management guidelines to help teachers teach without experiencing behavior interruptions,
- How to use open-ended responses to elicit higher achievement,

Kingore, B. (2008). *Teaching Without Nonsense*, 2nd ed. Austin, TX: Professional Associates Publishing.

- Rubrics that provide a standard for grading open-ended responses, and
- Several techniques that allow quick assessment when you only have a minute.

In this new edition, Section Two presents high-quality learning experiences that use high-level thinking and apply across the curriculum. They are organized alphabetically to allow logical access.

Students in today's classrooms represent diverse backgrounds, capabilities, interests, and learning profiles. Inasmuch as students demonstrate a wide-range of readiness levels, teachers tier instruction to layer the complexity of the skills and concepts they teach and insure that each student experiences continuous learning. In this second edition, every learning experience includes a comparison of ways to tier each task to simplify or increase the complexity and degree of support that is appropriate for students at different ages and levels of sophistication for that content.

Many of the learning experiences have Spanish translations for teachers to incorporate. These translations honor dual languages, provide examples in both English and Spanish, and save preparation time when working with ELL and bilingual students.

All of the learning experiences, templates, and examples are also provided on the interactive and customizable CD included with this book. Teachers and students are invited to use the CD to print off templates for skill applications and to create their own examples.

Purposes

The strategies and activities in this book:
- Promote students' long-term memory, high achievement, and integration of concepts and skills.
- Require less-intensive preparation time for teachers as they apply practical techniques and activities that stimulate students' thinking and achievement.
- Celebrate diversity in thinking as they encourage students to respond with multiple correct responses at different levels of complexity.
- Integrate multiple modalities to match more students with their best ways to learn.
- Relate the content being studied to students' lives and interests.
- Springboard students' discussions, summarizations, high-level thinking, and extensive writing about significant content information.
- Provide student and teacher choice through a variety of simple strategies and learning experiences that connect to a myriad of topics, content areas, and grade levels.
- Provide tools to assess students' accuracy, depth, and complexity of content.
- Replace worksheet activities requiring little thinking with mentally engaging tasks that challenge students to generate responses at high levels.
- Integrate instruction and assessment.

These learning experiences enable teachers to tier instruction to layer the complexity of the skills and concepts they teach and insure that each student experiences continuous learning.

Kingore, B. (2008). *Teaching Without Nonsense*, 2nd ed. Austin, TX: Professional Associates Publishing.

SECTION 1:
Effective, Efficient Instruction for High Achievement

TRANSLATING RESEARCH INTO EFFECTIVE PRACTICE

Effective instructional decisions and best practices extend from a solid research-base. The No Child Left Behind Act of 2001 and other state and district initiatives to improve education emphasize scientific research and research-based strategies as the basis for classroom practice. Research that relates to the requirements of these initiatives and learning standards is succinctly shared here to enable educators to more efficiently incorporate and document standards through applications of the learning experiences in this book.

Mental Engagement, Process Engagement, and Social-Emotional Connections

Brain research supports that achievement increases when learning experiences are designed to enhance students' mental engagement, process engagement, and social-emotional connections. Students' active involvement and personal processing of information are well documented to increase understanding and long-term memory as the brain seeks meaning and develops neural pathways that connect the unknown to what is known (Caine, Caine, Klimek, & McClintic, 2004; High/Scope Educational Research Foundation, 2005; Sousa, 2001; Sylwester, 2003). Teachers promote students' mental engagement through novelty, variety, and their enthusiasm for teaching combined with their personal love of the subject matter (Stronge, 2002). Skilled teachers engage students in metacognitive responses to help them develop a personal, conscious understanding of their learning process and increase long-term memory. Willis (2007a) emphasizes that at any point in a lesson, students should be able to answer the question: *Why are we learning this?*

Kingore, B. (2008). *Teaching Without Nonsense*, 2nd ed. Austin, TX: Professional Associates Publishing.

Social and emotional engagement is an additional factor in the brain's deeper understanding. The brain's understanding and retention increases when learning is enjoyable and directly relevant to students' lives, interests, and background experiences (Willis, 2007b; Wolfe, 2001). Conversely, stress limits the information flow to the higher cognitive networks and halts the learning process. Willis (2007b) asserts that when we scrub joy and comfort from learning environments, we risk distancing students from effective information processing and long-term memory storage.

Joyful learning does not mean facetious or merely entertaining activities. Master teachers increase social and emotional connections by knowing their students well, considering students' interests and modalities as they plan content applications, and weaving names of students, sports celebrities, and popular products such as an iPod™, into problem solving and learning situations. These teachers insure that hands-on activities also require minds-on applications and enhance learning within a rigorous, relevant curriculum (Wolfe, 2001).

The learning experiences shared in this book integrate mental engagement, process engagement, and social-emotional connections through high-appeal tasks that require students to generate responses as they interact. As Aristotle reportedly mused: *What we have to learn to do, we learn by doing.* The open-ended nature of these tasks increase students' opportunities for success through multiple modes of learning which then substantiates to them that their efforts result in achievement.

Research-Based Instructional Strategies and Practices

Research identifies summarization and similarities-differences as instructional strategies that promote the highest achievement gains (Marzano, Pickering, & Pollock, 2001). Since similarities and differences involve categorization, comparison, and analogous thinking, the learning experiences in this book weave these high-yield strategies into most lessons. Inasmuch as summarization assists long-term memory, many of these classroom experiences skillfully incorporate summarization as a closure to the tasks.

Recognizing-reinforcing effort, practice, nonlinguistic representations, and cooperative learning are additional strategies documented to provide the highest probability of enhancing student achievement (Marzano, Pickering, & Pollock, 2001; Wolfe, 2001). Combinations of these powerful strategies are applicable to both instruction and assessment in most tasks in this book. For example, the included learning experiences provide graphic organizers with applications that promote nonlinguistic as well as linguistic representations of content during instruction, practice, and evaluation. The appeal and versatility of these graphic tools enable them to be used multiple times in flexible group settings where recognizing and reinforcing effort occurs among

The goal is for every learning task to invite mental engagement, process engagement, and social-emotional connections that enable students to practice or extend content understanding.

Kingore, B. (2008). *Teaching Without Nonsense*, 2nd ed. Austin, TX: Professional Associates Publishing.

students as well as between the teacher and students.

High-level thinking is also vital to students' learning and long-term achievement (Anderson & Krathwohl, 2001; Erickson, 2007). Learning standards today demand more than memorization of facts and skills. With applications across the curriculum, these learning experiences are planned to progress students' thinking from beginning levels toward more complex levels because knowledge and skills are necessary but not sufficient elements of understanding for long-term retention and achievement (Shepard, 1997; Wiggins and McTighe, 2005; Willis 2006).

Higher achievement gains result when teachers instruct at levels that are challenging but attainable. Drawing upon the work of Vygotsky (1962), teachers scaffold instruction at students' zone of proximal development–the difference between a learner's current development level and the learner's emerging or potential level of development. Inasmuch as this zone varies, children must experience instruction at different levels (Berk & Winsler, 1995; National Reading Panel, 2000; Sousa, 2001).

Identifying and addressing instructional levels enable children to experience continuous learning. The brain makes sense of information by associating it with what it already knows. Splinter skills or short-term memory results when students memorize information but lack the background to hook it to. Thus, instruction produces higher achievement gains and encourages long-term memory when a teacher aims a lesson at the instructional level of the students in flexible-group settings (Berk & Winsler, 1995; High/Scope Educational Research Foundation, 2005; National Reading Panel, 2000; Sousa, 2001; Tomlinson, 2003).

The students in today's classrooms represent diverse backgrounds, capabilities, interests, and learning profiles. It is important for teachers to tier the complexity of learning tasks so each student is involved in the appropriate level of challenge that allows effort to result in achievement. Every learning experience in this book includes a comparison of ways to tier each task to simplify or increase the complexity and degree of support that is appropriate for students at different ages and levels of sophistication for that content.

Vocabulary

Vocabulary is directly related to comprehension and achievement (ASCD, 2006; Marzano, 2004; National Reading Panel, 2000). Current research documents that the vocabulary level of children entering first grade predicts their reading ability at the end of first grade as well as their eleventh grade reading comprehension (Marzano, 2004). Since reading comprehension influences the ability to learn any content area, vocabulary development emerges as a vital component in learning and achievement. The more words students know and can use appropriately, the better they can communicate ideas. Increasing vocabulary aids personal cognitive processing.

Research concludes that vocabulary develops when students read silently and independently, particularly non-fiction material

Kingore, B. (2008). *Teaching Without Nonsense*, 2nd ed. Austin, TX: Professional Associates Publishing.

in their areas of interest. It is also advanced by direct instruction incorporating meaningful context and multiple experiences with subject-specific vocabulary (ASCD, 2006). Additionally, drawing and creative dramatics of words and word meanings are found to increase vocabulary development and long-term memory (ASCD, 2006; Bull & Wittrock,1973; National Reading Panel, 2000; Wolfe, 2001). The applications in this book, including the class discussions, graphic organizers, comic drawings, and rubrics, consistently promote content-specific vocabulary and incorporate multiple modalities to provide more ways for students to process and learn vocabulary.

Current research documents that the vocabulary level of children entering first grade predicts both their reading ability at the end of first grade and their eleventh grade reading comprehension.

Teacher Effectiveness

Research continues to substantiate that the teacher is a significant component in students' level of achievement, directing the process that enables students to experience continuous learning (NAEYC& NAECS/SDE, 2003; Stronge, 2002). To illustrate, analysis of the Maryland School Assessment concluded that schools with high poverty and minorities produce thriving majorities of students scoring at the advanced levels on the state test when the schools are characterized by experienced, highly qualified teachers who stay at that school for years (Bowie, 2007). Two other characteristics of those high-achieving schools are extracurricular activities after school and advanced or gifted and talented classes using above-grade level materials.

Effective teachers respect and resound to learner differences. A teacher's enthusiasm for teaching and respect for students is contagious in classrooms as teachers seek fresh ways to engage students in meaningful learning applications. The learning experiences in this book emphasize diverse lesson choices to appeal to students' preferences, compliment different teaching styles, and minimize the intensity of preparation so teachers have more time and energy to teach.

Educators understand the value of research in planning effective instruction. They seek translations and specific applications of research through classroom experiences that optimize students' learning successes. The techniques and learning experiences in this book provide multiple, research-based applications to promote students' high achievement and joyful learning.

CLASSROOM MANAGEMENT WITHOUT NONSENSE

Teachers question how to manage the learning environment while differentiating instruction. The following are suggestions to simplify classroom management so energy is concentrated on instruction and learning instead of disruptive behavior.

- Notice and respond to students' positive behaviors. What we reinforce is what we communicate to students as important in our learning environment.

Kingore, B. (2008). *Teaching Without Nonsense*, 2nd ed. Austin, TX: Professional Associates Publishing.

SECTION 1: Effective, Efficient Instruction for High Achievement

- View each student as a puzzle to figure out rather than a problem to solve.

- Work with students to negotiate preferred personal behaviors, social interactions, and routines. Sharing ownership is a powerful technique in a classroom to insure students understand that teachers value them and their learning. Certainly, teachers can designate that some behaviors are non-negotiable and that some are required while still interactively communicating with the students to reach consensus on the set of guidelines agreeable to both students and teachers.

- Post the negotiated behaviors and working conditions so students and visitors understand and agree which behaviors are appropriate when working independently, in groups, or at learning stations.

- Limit the number of behavior rules for students to follow. Less is often more effective for students to remember and for teachers to monitor. I eventually established one rule that effectively responds to most student questions: *Do everything you can to help yourself and others learn.* When a behavior question emerges, I ask the student to explain how that would help everyone learn.

- Positive environments are bolstered by color, visual appeal, and mutual respect. An abundance of student displays of work and interests sets a student-centered atmosphere.

- Never do for students what they should do for themselves. In high-achieving, student-respected learning environments, teachers should not be working harder than their students. Or, as brain researchers would say: *Remember that the person doing the work is the one growing the dendrites* (Wolfe, 2001).

- If a student is absent, designate a classmate as a support assistant. The support assistant collects an extra copy of work as it is assigned and photocopies the class notes so a copy is ready for the absent student. When that student returns, the support assistant is able to provide the one-on-one attention needed to reorient the student. This process emphasizes student responsibility and collegiality as well as frees the teacher from additional details and paperwork.

Do everything you can to help yourself and others learn.

- Encourage students to use scrap paper as a planning sheet before they begin a task. This *sloppy-copy* encourages students to think and organize their work before they begin, and it frequently results in more complex, higher-quality outcomes.

- Increase active participation and mental engagement by having students quickly write responses before sharing their ideas in class. Say to them: *Take one minute and write why you think _____ is most important before we share ideas,* or *Write your best solution; then, we will compare with each other.*

Kingore, B. (2008). *Teaching Without Nonsense*, 2nd ed. Austin, TX: Professional Associates Publishing.

- Employ small groups for high achievement in skill applications. Research concludes that small, flexible groups of two to four result in the highest achievement gains (National Reading Panel, 2000). While it is unrealistic for all of instruction to occur in groups of two to four, this group size is feasible when asking students to engage in skill applications. Groups of two to four require more students to be on task. Larger groups can result in some students doing more of the work, even when teachers assign specific responsibilities to various group members.

- When multiple groups are working on a similar task, announce to the class: *Anything you hear from another group you may use!* Most groups then try to work very quietly to prevent others from hearing their ideas.

- Small group work provides a productive assessment time. As students work in groups, walk around the room making notes on a small writing pad. These notes accumulate into productive insights that guide instruction. Furthermore, some students are more motivated to stay on task because they are not sure what the teacher is recording. If a student asks: *What are you writing?* I always answer: *Important things I need to remember about you.*

- Students complete tasks at different rates. Post a set of Now Whats–productive, alternative tasks students select when they are finished, such as silent reading, computer applications, playing a math or vocabulary game, and continuing an art project. Negotiate a list of appropriate options with students so they have meaningful choices as others continue to work. Begin with a short list of two to four choices and add others as ideas develop and students demonstrate their ability to take responsibility for their actions. With Now Whats, students do not need to interrupt the teacher or disrupt other students.

- Make every moment a teachable moment—in the hallway, on the playground, waiting for the bell, standing in line, or during transitions. Enjoy spontaneous applications, delight in even brief learning interactions, and infect students with the love of learning together.

- Acknowledge that there can be differences between teaching the lesson and students learning the targeted content. It is counterproductive for teachers to say: *I taught it; these kids just don't remember it.* Teachers can broadcast information to a class, but they have not taught until the students demonstrate understanding of the concepts and skills through their applications. This is what Erickson refers to as KUD: ***K**now, **U**nderstand and are able to **D**o* (Erickson, 2007).

- When working with students who are more challenging and difficult to motivate, successful teachers change approaches knowing that multiple pathways increase access to learning.

Remember that the person doing the work is the one growing the dendrites (Wolfe, 2001).

Kingore, B. (2008). *Teaching Without Nonsense*, 2nd ed. Austin, TX: Professional Associates Publishing.

OPEN-ENDED TASKS FOR MULTIPLE LEARNING APPLICATIONS

Research supports that a wider range of students' capabilities are addressed through using an array of learning tasks beyond simple fill-in-the-blank responses (Hertzog, 1998; High/Scope Educational Research Foundation, 2005; Wolfe, 2001). Tasks requiring single-correct-answers limit students' opportunities to incorporate multiple-modalities and high-levels of thinking in their responses.

Open-ended tasks are flexible learning experiences that enable students' processes and products to be as individual as the students. Open-ended does not imply that quality is not important or that any response is acceptable. Rather, these tasks acknowledge that more than one answer and more than one procedure is possible. As a correct response emerges, students can build upon that response, develop additional possibilities, bring their individuality to each learning opportunity, and document different levels of expertise and understanding. Hence, open-ended tasks incorporate challenge and elicit complexity (Tomlinson, 2003). While not appropriate in all learning situations, open-ended tasks allow more students to be successful by honoring diverse modalities, a range of ideas, varied learning processes, and multiple levels of understanding rather than rewarding only the simple, memorized answers.

Many open-ended learning experiences take the form of graphic organizers that prompt understanding of relationships through a visual, nonlinguistic as well as linguistic representation and organization of information. Seek open-ended tasks with the following characteristics.

> **CHARACTERISTICS OF OPEN-ENDED TASKS**
> ✓ Apply to multiple topics, grade levels, and content areas
> ✓ Promote diverse levels of thinking, depth, and complexity
> ✓ Increase success for all students
> ✓ Are used multiple times and applied in multiple ways
> ✓ Save instruction time
> ✓ Provide effective learning-center and small-group tasks with less teacher preparation or direction
> ✓ Increase students' comfort level for different responses and ways of learning

The learning experiences, applications, and variations provided in this book exemplify these characteristics. Since teachers express frustration about not having enough time to accomplish all that is required when enabling students to achieve, it is significant that open-ended tasks save instruction time. Specifically, when students know how to do a task, teachers save the class time it previously took to teach the process. They can immediately proceed with the specific application for the current lesson. Furthermore, teachers save time because multiple applications of open-ended learning experiences demand less teacher preparation or direction. Once students are experienced with Venn diagrams, for example, a teacher can readily lift the challenge through students' independent applications. *Use the Venn diagram*

Kingore, B. (2008). *Teaching Without Nonsense*, 2nd ed. Austin, TX: Professional Associates Publishing.

in the math learning station to compare and contrast fractions and decimals. Conclude with a statement defending or rejecting the need for students to learn fractions in our digital age.

Compile a list of open-ended learning experiences that are appropriate for students' developmental levels and effectively integrate the targeted concepts and skills. It is advantageous if these tasks are also compatible to teaching style and multiple applications.

A running list of open-ended learning experiences is a valued tool to maximize the application of effective learning opportunities and minimize teacher preparation. When preparing lessons, quickly determine the most relevant ways for students to demonstrate their applications of skills and concepts by skimming the list and selecting one or more applicable learning experiences. Most teachers immediately find connections they can use.

Expand the effectiveness of this tool by jotting down ideas to elaborate the specific applications that come to mind while skimming the list. Typically, this tool helps teachers deftly generate ideas that enhance and vary students' learning opportunities.

GRADING OPEN-ENDED RESPONSES

Rubrics are the evaluation tool of choice to assess open-ended learning experiences.

- **Rubrics are guidelines** to quality.
  They challenge students to think about quality work and plan how to succeed.
- **Rubrics are standards** for evaluation.
  They provide a clearer standard for the proficiencies and deficiencies of students' work to more accurately and fairly determine grades.

A rubric is helpful when communicating learning goals and evaluation decisions to students and families. A rubric lists criteria, such as the quality of information, research, thinking levels, and communication skills, that represent the main ideas of the learning experience and explain what is expected at each level of proficiency. Avoid excessive emphasis on neatness or appearance that implies to students that flash value is more important than content.

Generic rubrics are designed to be used in multiple applications throughout the year rather than require teachers to develop a separate rubric for each learning task. Repeated applications of a generic rubric help students develop a language of achievement

OPEN-ENDED LEARNING EXPERIENCES
- Venn Diagram
- KWL, KWLS, and KWRDL
- Acrostic
- Alphabet Time
- Concept Map
- Thinking Map
- Story Map
- Relation Chart
- Sentence Cents
- Word Map
-
-
-
-

Kingore, B. (2008). *Teaching Without Nonsense*, 2nd ed. Austin, TX: Professional Associates Publishing.

and consistently build students' understanding of the continuum from a minimal to highly proficient learning response. Generic rubrics benefit teachers. They save time so teachers can concentrate on teaching students to understand these criteria and extend proficiency. Begin with a generic rubric and modify that rubric as students progress.

Rubrics are applicable to all grade levels, and four generic rubrics for open-ended learning experiences are provided. Each represents a different tier of complexity to respond to the level and sophistication of students. The pictorial rubric is appropriate for some ELL and young children. The next tier combines pictures with a minimum of text for developing readers. The third and fourth tiers increase the readability level and complexity of expectations appropriate for students with more skills. To increase learning value, assessment feedback must cause students' to think and allow for self-adjustment (Leahy, Lyon, Thompson, & Wiliam, 2005). Each rubric concludes with a space for students' reflections and action plan that they check (✓) and explain: *Satisfied, Refine, Revise, Retry,* or *Extend.*

Experienced teachers recommend modeling higher and lower examples of any open-ended response to guide students' understanding of quality. Include simple to more complex correct-product samples for comparison so students understand that there are multiple ways to successfully complete the task and gain confidence to think differently than others. Then, provide the most applicable generic rubric to guide students in an assessment discussion that evolves into grading the product samples using a rubric.

Initially, make evaluation with a rubric a brief and concrete process by focusing on two products representing vastly different levels of quality. Discuss and clarify the words and illustrations on each proficiency level so students are not lost in the language on the rubric. When appropriate, extend students' product evaluation and comparative thinking by comparing products that narrow the range of the differences in proficiencies. Discuss the value of effort, and ensure that students understand that teachers design learning experiences to guide students' learning. *It is my job to plan learning experiences you can do successfully that will help you practice and extend learning. It is your job to do all you can to help yourself learn.*

Continue developing students' use of rubrics by having students work in pairs to complete different evaluations. This application increases students' opportunity to use assessment language and is engaging as students are often more motivated when evaluating others' work than their own. Peer assessment should emphasize practicing and refining evaluation with rubrics and providing feedback to peers. Students should not be giving other students grades that will be reported to parents or administrators (Leahy, Lyon, Thompson, & Wiliam, 2005).

As students' evaluation expertise increases, have them use a rubric to model product evaluation with parents at home or during student-involved conferences. Eventually, students are able to assume a leading role in developing the rubrics used to evaluate their learning tasks.

Kingore, B. (2008). *Teaching Without Nonsense*, 2nd ed. Austin, TX: Professional Associates Publishing.

OPEN-ENDED LEARNING EXPERIENCE

NAME _____ DATE _____

TASK _____

Information	Picture	a worm / wiggle — Picture and words	Worms help us. They mix the soil. They fertilize it. — Picture and sentences
POINTS:			
Thinking			
POINTS:			
Vocabulary, Punctuation, and Capitalization	hear the dog	Hear the dog he is loud.	Do you hear that little dog? He is very loud!
POINTS:			
Worked	Did not work	Started and worked	Started, worked and finished on time.
POINTS:			

TOTAL POINTS: _____

Developed using the Rubric Generator in Kingore, B. (2007). *Assessment,* 4th ed.

OPEN-ENDED LEARNING EXPERIENCE

NAME _____ DATE _____

TASK _____

Information	Simple Limited understanding Points _____	Developed Correct Basic facts Points _____	Detailed Elaborated Interesting information Points _____
POINTS:			
Communication	Mistakes Confusing Points _____	Mostly correct Points _____	Skillful Powerful words and sentences Points _____
POINTS:			
Thinking	Knows Points _____	Understands Applies ideas Points _____	Analyzes Explains Unique ideas Points _____
POINTS:			
Neat and Organized	Not neat Hard to follow Points _____	Attractive Organized Clear sequence Points _____	Eye-catching Well organized Fluent Clarifies content Points _____
POINTS:			

TOTAL POINTS: _____

Developed using the Rubric Generator in Kingore, B. (2007). *Assessment,* 4th ed.

OPEN-ENDED LEARNING EXPERIENCE

NAME _____ DATE _____

ASSIGNMENT _____

	Information	Communication	Organization & Appearance	Thinking
Getting started	Little information; not accurate	Serious errors make it hard to understand	Unorganized; unable to follow; not neat	Knows basic facts
On the right track	Basic facts; needs elaboration	Frequent errors but readable; emerging skills; uses simple words and phrases	Hard to follow but sequenced; needs more attention to detail	Understands and applies ideas
Got it	Develops topic well; includes most key ideas and concepts; some substantiation	Appropriate in _ capitalization _ punctuation _ spelling _ complete sentences _ grammar Interesting, varied words; descriptive	Organized; a clear sequence; neat and attractive	Considers issues; compares; explains
Wow!	In-depth information; well supported ideas; elaborates	Skillful application in _ capitalization _ punctuation _ spelling _ complete sentences _ grammar Advanced terms and multiple-syllable words	Skillfully planned, organized, and sequenced; fluent; careful attention to detail; eye-catching	Evaluates evidence and alternatives; original

Total Points / **Comments:**

Student Action: ❏ Satisfied ❏ Refine ❏ Revise ❏ Retry ❏ Extend

Reflection:

Developed using the Rubric Generator in Kingore, B. (2007). *Assessment,* 4th ed.

OPEN-ENDED LEARNING EXPERIENCE

NAME _____ DATE _____

ASSIGNMENT _____

	Information	Communication	Organization & Appearance	Thinking
Below standard	Little knowledge evident; reiterates facts without complete accuracy	Serious errors makes reading and understanding difficult flawed vocabulary	Unclear; lacks organization; not neat; little care evident	Vague; basic
Apprentice	Provides basic facts; lacks key ideas; valid but little depth	Frequent errors present but content is readable; emerging skills; appropriate but basic vocabulary	Attempts to organize and sequence but is hard to follow adequate appearance	General understanding; focuses on single issue; limited examination of evidence
Proficient	Well developed major ideas and concepts; some appropriate substantiation; explores beyond facts	Minimal errors; mechanics and spelling are typical and appropriate for grade level; descriptive language is appropriate with elaboration	Organized effectively; a good beginning and ending; a clear sequence; well structured; attractive and visually appealing	Understands scope of problem and more than one of the issues; conclusion reflects examination of information
Exceeding	Relates in-depth knowledge of concepts and relationships; well supported; examines issues	Product is enhanced by the skillful application of mechanics; fluid; above expectations; interesting; uses specific terminology; precise, advanced language; rich imagery	Coherent; skillfully planned; logically sequenced and organized to communicate well; eye-catching; aesthetically pleasing; beyond expectations	Clearly understands scope and issues; conclusions based upon thorough examination of evidence; explores reasonable alternatives; evaluates consequences; original

Total Points   **Comments:**
    /

Student Action: ❏ Satisfied   ❏ Refine   ❏ Revise   ❏ Retry   ❏ Extend

Reflection:

Developed using the Rubric Generator in Kingore, B. (2007). *Assessment,* 4th ed.

QUICK ASSESSMENT TECHNIQUES: WHEN YOU ONLY HAVE A MINUTE

Assessment is valuable when it results in feedback and information that guide instruction and benefit students. To promote achievement, insightful teachers use assessment to modify instruction as they teach rather than merely determine at the conclusion of a unit who has and has not learned. As McTighe and O"Connor (2005) assert: *Waiting until the end of a teaching period to find out how well students have learned is simply too late* (p. 10).

Effective assessment guides instruction and benefits students.

Assessment becomes interpretive rather than just evaluative when teachers listen for what they can conclude about the students' thinking instead of listening only for the correct answer (Leahy, Lyon, Thompson, & Wiliam, 2005). Using assessment interpretively empowers teachers with information they use to adjust instruction to meet students' learning needs.

Consider the following techniques to immediately access information and feedback that guide interpretive assessment. Some of these simple-to-implement techniques are effective as a pre-assessment, some work best for formative assessment, some are most effective as a closure, some are adaptable for multiple assessment junctures, and all are effective when time is a premium.

Handy 1-5 + Wave

Students use their hand to indicate their interests, preferences, and needs for depth or more guided practice. Extending their arm in the air, they hold up one to five fingers to indicate a degree of low to high. A wave indicates the highest degree. For instance, when prioritizing how many examples and how much emphasis to expend on subparts of a topic, each student in the class exhibits personal preferences by showing one for a lesser need and four or five fingers for a higher interest or need. The technique is also used during a lesson as the teacher stops and requests that students indicate their level of understanding.

This assessment is more valid when students are required to close their eyes. Then individuals are less likely to be influenced by peer responses and more inclined to indicate individual opinions.

OPEN-ENDED ASSESSMENTS

1. Handy 1-5 + wave
2. OUT
3. Minute Paper
4. Muddiest Point
5. Individual Response Boards
6. Error Investigation
7. Analogies
8. Feedback Number
9. Name Cards and Name Sticks-Quick Quiz
10. Topic Talk and Switch

Kingore, B. (2008). *Teaching Without Nonsense*, 2nd ed. Austin, TX: Professional Associates Publishing.

This technique can be applied during a lesson or as a closure when posing questions with multiple-choice answers and requiring students to exhibit the number for the correct answer. Scan responses and quickly judge whether to move on or reteach-clarify content.

OUT

OUT is an oral review technique that is useful as a closure when time is short. In pairs, students review the content to develop responses to each key prompt. As a whole group, students share and compare ideas on their lists to reach a consensus of the most significant points.

Each letter of the technique represents different aspects of the lesson. The *O* stands for objective and asks students to restate the purpose of the lesson. The *U* is for understandings and prompts students to share the big ideas or new content that was addressed and the personal connections students made. The *T* is for tips and provides students an opportunity to analyze their learning process and express ideas to pursue, suggestions to consider, or strategies to use. Teachers assess students' responses to interpret their acquisition of information and concepts.

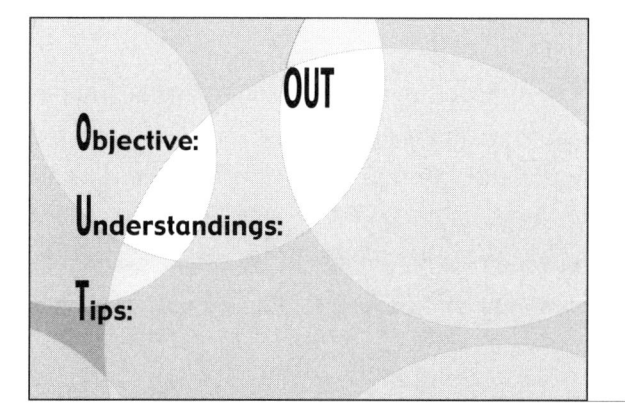

OUT

Objective:

Understandings:

Tips:

Minute Paper

A Minute Paper invites students to write a brief reflection about content (Cross, 1998). In this combination of self-reflection and Exit Tickets, the teacher poses a metacognitive question to which students have a minute to quickly write their response. Teachers may elect to extend the time to two or three minutes as a better match to children's capabilities. This technique is most motivating when the teacher uses a stop watch or second hand on a watch for accurate time measurement.

The emphasis is on content rather than spelling or handwriting. Typically, students' responses are collected for the teacher's review but also function as a discussion generator to guide students toward a consensus of key points. Add to the following questions as potential minute paper prompts.

MINUTE PAPER QUESTIONS

- *What was our learning objective and what did you do to learn it?*
- *How did you figure this out?*
- *What is the most important thing that you learned while working on this?*
- *What is one thing you understand well enough to teach to someone else?*
- *What is a connection you made to this information?*
- *What analogy can you create to explain this?*
- _____

Kingore, B. (2008). *Teaching Without Nonsense*, 2nd ed. Austin, TX: Professional Associates Publishing.

Muddiest Point

The Muddiest Point is a variation of the Minute Paper (Cross, 1998). To clarify any confusion or misconceptions, students are asked for a quick reflection to describe problems and concerns they have with the content.

As with the Minute Paper, emphasize content and students' responses; then, collect the responses for review. The information signals reteaching needs and guides flexible group placements. The following questions illustrate potential prompts.

> **MUDDIEST POINT QUESTIONS**
>
> - *What you are most confused about in class?*
> - *What part causes the most trouble?*
> - *What problem are you having with this?*
> - *What is the hardest thing for you to do with this?*
> - *What is an unanswered question you leave class with today?*
> - _____
> - _____
> - _____

Individual Response Boards

Individual response boards are small chalkboards, dry-erase boards, or laminated index cards that students write on and hold up at the teacher's request to demonstrate understanding. Teachers can instantly view students' understanding or misconceptions by noting which students quickly record the correct answer, who looks around for help before writing, and who needs reteaching or additional practice to reach understanding.

The strategy is simple to use and encourages students to remain mentally engaged instead of mentally disconnecting as when only one student responds to a question. It is best used with short-answer, often single word responses to account for differences in students' writing speeds.

Error Investigation

Provide students with key content examples or statements that have errors for students to identify and explain. As a closure task, inform the class that there is misinformation or mistakes in the content without telling them the total number of errors. Working in pairs for two minutes, students determine which errors they can identify and explain how to correct. This assessment technique is engaging, as many students respond enthusiastically to finding others' errors. After two minutes, ask students to share and compare what they found.

Error Investigation is particularly applicable for math problems, a science process, historical information, story retelling, and vocabulary or spelling skills. The novelty of flawed information is an effective device to stimulate students' attention to key concepts and skills.

Kingore, B. (2008). *Teaching Without Nonsense*, 2nd ed. Austin, TX: Professional Associates Publishing.

Analogies

Analogies are a format to relate similarities and differences—the most significant strategy for effectively increasing student achievement (Marzano, 2001). They are a useful assessment tool with applications across the curriculum as students must understand all of the components in an analogy in order to create or complete the relationship. To assess understanding and promote memory, the teacher poses incomplete analogies about the topic. Students are asked to individually write their responses on a response board or discuss the analogy in pairs and then share their best answers.

Direct analogies are thought-provoking tools that can tease out topic-related inferences and assess more in-depth or complex information. For example, ask students to pose and explain an analogy expressing how an historical event being studied is like a part of a house or how a scientist is like an item in the laboratory. *The industrial revolution is like the front porch of our cultural house because it was an entrance into contemporary human social history.*

Feedback Number

A feedback number guides the pace and level of instruction as well as benefits students by inviting students to provide feedback to the teacher regarding their level of confidence in their learning. The class discusses a scale similar to the example provided here. After completing an assignment, students write a feedback number under their name on their paper. This information is not intended to

---

ANALOGIES

- Triangle is to three as square is to _____.
- Circumference is to circle as perimeter is to _____.
- Plants are to carbon dioxide as mammals are to _____.
- Core is to earth as nucleus is to _____.
- Little Red Riding Hood is to character as forest is to _____.
- Paul Bunyon is to tall tale as Gilly Hopkins is to _____.
- Colorado is to mountains as Alaska is to _____.
- Manifest Destiny is to a covered wagon in Oregon as isolationism is to _____ in _____.

FEEDBACK NUMBER

- ❏ 5 I own this! I understand information and connections beyond what was taught.
- ❏ 4 I get it! I understand what was taught and can do this without making mistakes.
- ❏ 3 I know some parts. I don't understand all of it.
- ❏ 2 I understand some of this. I need some help to do this well.
- ❏ 1 I need another way to learn this.

Kingore, B. (2008). *Teaching Without Nonsense*, 2nd ed. Austin, TX: Professional Associates Publishing.

affect a grade; rather, it guides instruction by clarifying the students' perspective of their learning needs. It helps instructors reach decisions about which students would benefit from reteaching, a different approach, continuing guided practice, or extensions.

Name Cards and Name Sticks-Quick Quiz

Every student's name is written on an index card or on a Popsicle™ stick. The idea is that the teacher randomly draws a name after asking a question. When the question is answered, the name is put back in the pile and the names are sorted again for the next random selection. All students know that they need to stay mentally engaged as any one of them may be selected to respond.

Some teachers praise the fairness of this approach. Others express concern about students feeling put on the spot. I found it most successful as a quick quiz, drawing one name to answer my posed question and then a second name to respond to the student's answer. Additional names can be drawn when further elaboration is needed.

Topic Talk and Switch

The teacher organizes students in pairs or trios to briefly discuss a designated topic or process, such as how to conduct a science experiment or complete and check a math problem. The students stand, face each other, and determine who goes first. At the teacher's signal, one student begins discussing the topic until the teacher calls, *Switch*. Then, the second student in each pair picks up the discussion in mid-sentence and continues talking until switch is called again. Encourage students to use the most specific vocabulary related to the topic. Use a stopwatch or second hand on a watch to keep this interaction moving along at a brisk pace.

Topic Talk and Switch can be an interactive application of reading comprehension. The pair of students retell a story or event in sequence as a third student uses a checklist of the story content as an assessment tool and checks off each correct event or detail the pair of students incorporates.

With this quick assessment, student motivation to succeed is increased by fast pacing and by holding students accountable for learning. Circulate among the groups, coaching and informally assessing by writing brief notes. Switching and requiring students to continue mid-sentence increases students' need to actively listen and respond to each other's information. As a conclusion, randomly draw one or more students' names and ask each to summarize their discussion.

Kingore, B. (2008). *Teaching Without Nonsense*, 2nd ed. Austin, TX: Professional Associates Publishing.

SECTION 2:
Learning Experiences

GUIDELINES FOR SUCCESS

Modeling for Success

To maximize learning, effective teachers model how to complete each new learning process or activity. Students need to experience success with each activity before they can proceed by themselves. Students can not be expected to work responsibly and independently when they are uncertain how to successfully complete the work.

Additionally, students benefit from support and practice when learning how to identify the important information and the relationships among the concepts. Deciding what information is important and how to most effectively organize that data is a vital process that requires high-level thinking and active involvement as it guides students to construct meaning and promote long-term memory.

Flexible Grouping

The learning experiences shared in this book are applicable in a variety of group settings. They can be introduced and modeled as a whole class. With experience, however, these tasks are more effective when completed in small groups, pairs, or individual-student settings to increase mental engagement and match individual learning capabilities. When students work in small groups, interaction, high-level thinking, and negotiation become critical components that more accurately represent the content mastery and perspective of each student.

Students as Producers

With experience, students can apply these learning tasks without direct teacher instruction. Some students may build upon the provided examples and begin to construct their own adaptations. Students demonstrate higher levels of productivity when they move from

---

Kingore, B. (2008). *Teaching Without Nonsense*, 2nd ed. Austin, TX: Professional Associates Publishing.

consumers responding to assignments to producers who create their own models. A wider variety of responses at different levels of understanding and complexity result when students generate their own examples than when teachers produce the problems or examples for students to complete.

Mental Engagement

These learning experiences are designed to mentally engage students in learning. Mental engagement means that students are consciously alert and involved. It is often stimulated through novelty and variety. Students who are mentally engaged are seldom bored as active involvement increases their learning and personal connections to the content. The goal is for most of the students to be mentally engaged most of the time.

Process Engagement

Students benefit from time to reflect and acknowledge their learning process and results. These experiences encourage students to evaluate their involvement and processes. Indeed, personal processing of information increases understanding and retention.

Social, Emotional Connections

With pleasurable classroom activities, the brain releases dopamine, a neurotransmitter that stimulates the memory centers and promotes focused attention. Hence, positive emotional experiences enable students to form more favorable associations toward what they learn and promote long-term memory (Willis, 2007).

Multiple Modalities

Students experience higher achievement when instruction responds to multiple modes of learning and how students learn best (Campbell & Campbell, 1999; Sternberg & Grigorenko, 1998; Willis, 2006). Teachers integrate multiple modalities because the more ways information is introduced to the brain the more dendritic pathways of access are created to enhance memory (Willis, 2006).

High-Level Thinking and Responses

High-level thinking is required for every student. While advanced students may exhibit high-level thinking responses most of the time, all students benefit from multiple opportunities for high-level thinking. The open-ended nature of the tasks presented in this book challenge students to think beyond simple, correct answers to analyze, synthesize, and evaluate content.

Multiple Content and Topic Applications

Activities with multiple application opportunities help integrate and practice the learning standards, content, and skills for which teachers are responsible. Successful teachers do not use instructional time for activities that are only fun to do. The goal is for every learning task to invite mental engagement, process engagement, and social-emotional connections that enable students to practice or extend content understanding. Use the learning experiences that follow instead of simpler, low-level thinking tasks.

Kingore, B. (2008). *Teaching Without Nonsense*, 2nd ed. Austin, TX: Professional Associates Publishing.

Acrostic

Grade Levels: K-12

Kindergartners complete this task with adult facilitation.

An acrostic learning experience:
- Provides a simple-to-prepare activity that connects to a myriad of topics, content areas, and skills.
- Serves as a springboard for topic discussions, vocabulary development, and review.
- Encourages students' application, analysis, and synthesis.
- Promotes conceptual thinking more than recall or simple thinking.
- Serves as an assessment tool to assess the accuracy, depth, and complexity of information.

Acrostics display a key term, concept, or topic label and use each letter of that word to guide relationships and organize connected ideas. They are useful in primary classrooms because they reinforce grapheme-phoneme relationships as students investigate topics. They are equally valued in upper elementary and secondary classrooms as they encourage students to generate key facts, examples, or attributes of a topic.

Introduce what an acrostic is and how to complete one by modeling the process using a well-know adult's name and determining words about that person for each letter of the person's name. Teachers often prepare an acrostic using their names to personalize the task with their classes. Then, ask students to

Acrostic

Joker; a joyful juvenile
Outside; often outside playing soccer
Scientist; sometimes serious, sometimes silly, seldom silent
Happy, honest, helpful (usually), hardworking (usually), hates bullies

Josh
Second grade

Kingore, B. (2008). *Teaching Without Nonsense*, 2nd ed. Austin, TX: Professional Associates Publishing.

Kingore, B. (2008). *Teaching Without Nonsense*, 2nd ed. Austin, TX: Professional Associates Publishing.

write their first name as an acrostic and complete that acrostic with information they want everyone to know about them. As an example, Josh completes an example for his name, uses a thesaurus, and combines images from the Comic Characters activity to create his illustration. To demonstrate how students change as learners, consider having students complete a second acrostic for their names at the end of the year to compare with their earlier composition. Acrostics readily adapt to multiple languages by using concept words or key terms in languages other than English.

Acrostics are a useful tool for prompting vocabulary development. When using acrostics, increase students' awareness of the vocabulary of the field by challenging them to apply the most appropriate and specific terminology rather than only simple words.

Variations

- One appealing feature of acrostic is the multiple variations of the task that are possible when used as a learning experience. A telestich and double acrostic are examples of easy-to-implement variations to promote students' continued interest in acrostics. Specifically, a regular acrostic places the concept word as the beginning letter of each response, a telestich places the concept word as the last letter of each response, and a double acrostic repeats the concept word so that each response must begin and end with the letters in the concept word. Students are more successful with double acrostic when each response is a sentence instead of a single word. While all three versions require analysis and content knowledge, telestich and double acrostic are harder to compete.

Acrostic

T_____
H_____
I_____
N_____
K_____

Telestich

_____T
_____H
_____I
_____N
_____K

Double Acrostic

T_____T
H_____H
I_____I
N_____N
K_____K

- Typically, each line of an acrostic is completed as a single word response, a list of several words, or a phrase. When a teacher wishes to reinforce sentence structure and encourage more elaboration of information, require students to develop each line as one or more complete sentences. The fractions example is an acrostic developed with elaborated content.

- The organization and thinking challenge is even more complex when an acrostic is completed as continuous text which is read like a paragraph, as in the astronaut example that follows.

Kingore, B. (2008). *Teaching Without Nonsense*, 2nd ed. Austin, TX: Professional Associates Publishing.

SECTION 2: Learning Experiences

Continuous text variations require students to engage in extensive analysis and planning to structure information in that form. The friends acrostic shared later in this section is a continuous text example that requires students to demonstrate the theme of a book and use that theme as the prompt to summarize the story.

- A grammar acrostic is one example that applies specific skills in an acrostic. With a grammar acrostic, multiple concept words can be used, but all of the responses must be a designated part of speech. For example, when a group is analyzing a historical event, the event becomes the concept word, and the response for each letter must be an adjective that is relevant to that event.

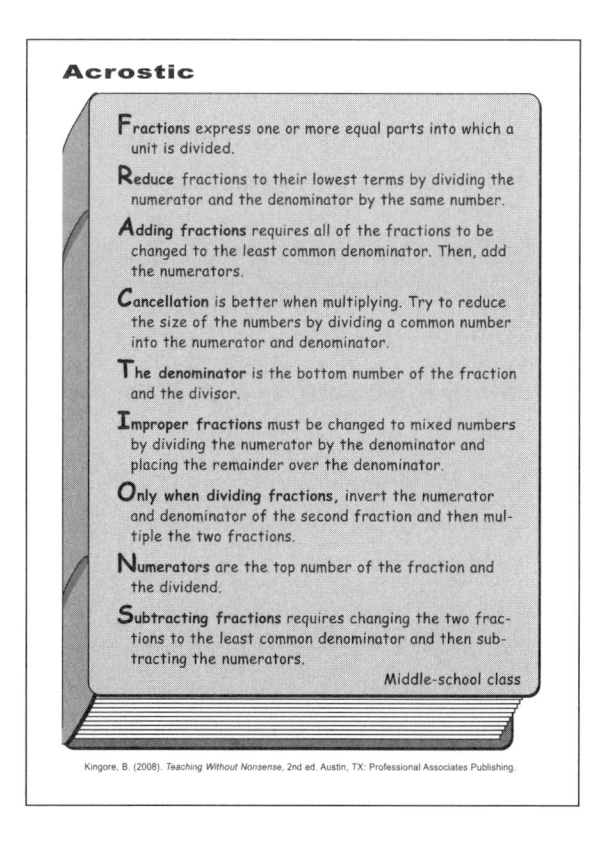

Acrostic

Fractions express one or more equal parts into which a unit is divided.

Reduce fractions to their lowest terms by dividing the numerator and the denominator by the same number.

Adding fractions requires all of the fractions to be changed to the least common denominator. Then, add the numerators.

Cancellation is better when multiplying. Try to reduce the size of the numbers by dividing a common number into the numerator and denominator.

The denominator is the bottom number of the fraction and the divisor.

Improper fractions must be changed to mixed numbers by dividing the numerator by the denominator and placing the remainder over the denominator.

Only when dividing fractions, invert the numerator and denominator of the second fraction and then multiple the two fractions.

Numerators are the top number of the fraction and the dividend.

Subtracting fractions requires changing the two fractions to the least common denominator and then subtracting the numerators.

Middle-school class

Kingore, B. (2008). *Teaching Without Nonsense*, 2nd ed. Austin, TX: Professional Associates Publishing.

- As another complex application, challenge students to develop a process acrostic. This variation requires extensive analysis, content understanding, and related vocabulary as students have to figure out how to respond to each letter in the concept word in such a way that they explain the process in sequence. Retelling a science experiment, explaining how to use a piece of equipment, describing a life cycle, or explaining how to apply a math strategy are examples of process acrostic.

Acrostic

Across the universe, across

Space, the lucky man in a

Teal blue flight suit is

Ready to uncover the heavens'

Own mystery,

Not for himself, but for the

Americans, his people.

Unto them, he is willing

To risk his life for joyous knowledge.

Amy, middle school

Kingore, B. (2008). *Teaching Without Nonsense*, 2nd ed. Austin, TX: Professional Associates Publishing.

- An acrostic can be used as an assessment tool at the conclusion of a topic of study. Individual students respond to a key concept word with ideas that express the depth of their knowledge and understanding. Motivate students to aim beyond simple but accurate information by challenging them to demonstrate the most important information they know. A teacher might prompt this depth by

Kingore, B. (2008). *Teaching Without Nonsense*, 2nd ed. Austin, TX: Professional Associates Publishing.

stating: *I am not interested in simple, cute, or funny responses right now. Show me the meat. Include the most significant and sophisticated information you can.*

Options for Implementation

Modeling for Depth and Complexity

Help students understand what depth and complexity of information look and sound like. Partially complete a simple and more complex version of an acrostic before showing the products to students. After discussing the differences between the simpler and more complex responses, facilitate as students work together to construct in-depth and complex information for the letters that are not completed on the more complex version.

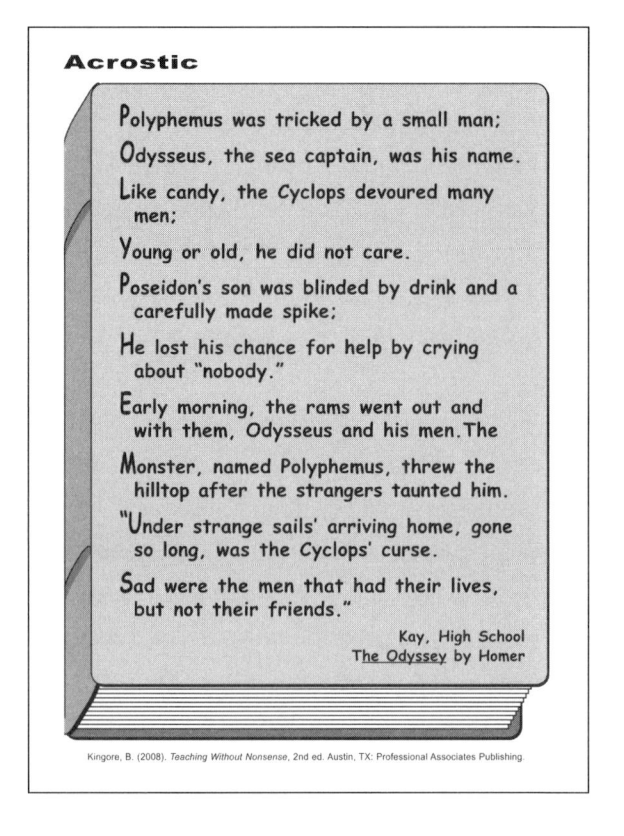

Acrostic

Polyphemus was tricked by a small man;
Odysseus, the sea captain, was his name.
Like candy, the Cyclops devoured many men;
Young or old, he did not care.
Poseidon's son was blinded by drink and a carefully made spike;
He lost his chance for help by crying about "nobody."
Early morning, the rams went out and with them, Odysseus and his men. The
Monster, named Polyphemus, threw the hilltop after the strangers taunted him.
"Under strange sails' arriving home, gone so long, was the Cyclops' curse.
Sad were the men that had their lives, but not their friends."

Kay, High School
<u>The Odyssey</u> by Homer

Kingore, B. (2008). *Teaching Without Nonsense*, 2nd ed. Austin, TX: Professional Associates Publishing.

Small-Group Cooperative Task

Groups of two or three students are each assigned one letter of the target acrostic. Each group then researches provided materials and prepares two content connections that fit their assigned letter. Having students prepare two connections compensates for possible duplication from other groups who might apply the same key point to their letter. Have the groups copy their connections on strips cut from overhead transparencies. Then, the ideas can be effectively and efficiently shared or reorganized on the overhead without extra recopying time.

As the whole class participates, the students discuss the content and determine the best information to use to complete the class acrostic. In this manner, the acrostic serves as an excellent review technique. The previously shared fractions acrostic example was completed as a cooperative task.

One a Day

Use an acrostic as a continuing element and daily closure technique during a topic of study. The class works together to complete one letter each day, integrating the concepts and information they learned at that time. Emphasize concept connections rather than working to complete the letters in the word in order.

Kingore, B. (2008). *Teaching Without Nonsense*, 2nd ed. Austin, TX: Professional Associates Publishing.

Error Analysis

Display an acrostic with three or more information errors. As a closure task, inform the class that there is misinformation in the acrostic without telling them the total number of errors. Challenge students to work in pairs or trios for two minutes to see how many of the errors they can identify and explain to other classmates how to correct. Many students respond enthusiastically to the novelty of finding others' errors.

Individual Applications

Acrostics are an easy-to-use, alternative learning task when individual students are organizing researched information or responding to a story. Since students decree that is it not fair if one student's acrostic concept word is longer or shorter, consider using generalizable terms such as *research* and *great book* that apply equally well to any topic or book.

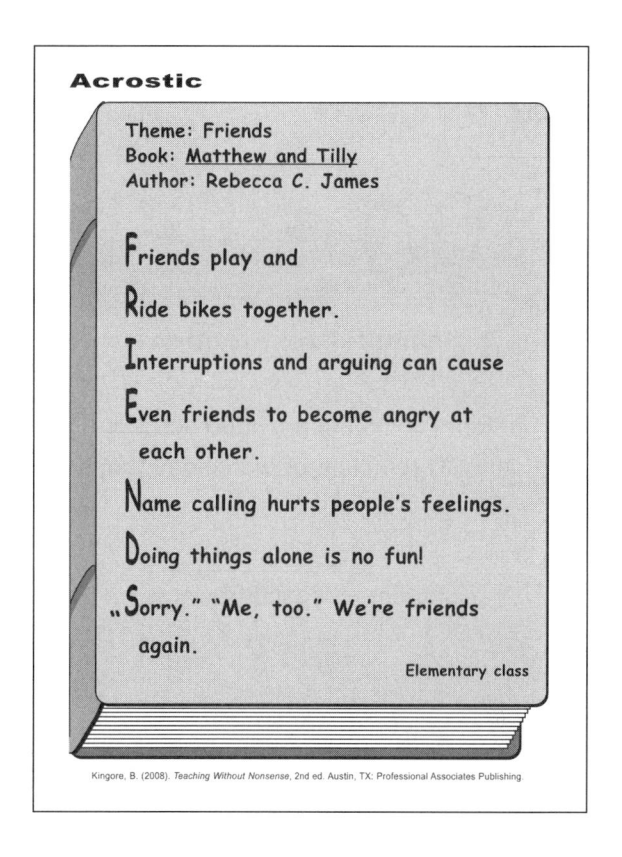

Acrostic

Theme: Friends
Book: Matthew and Tilly
Author: Rebecca C. James

Friends play and
Ride bikes together.
Interruptions and arguing can cause
Even friends to become angry at each other.
Name calling hurts people's feelings.
Doing things alone is no fun!
"Sorry." "Me, too." We're friends again.

Elementary class

Kingore, B. (2008). *Teaching Without Nonsense*, 2nd ed. Austin, TX: Professional Associates Publishing.

Kingore, B. (2008). *Teaching Without Nonsense*, 2nd ed. Austin, TX: Professional Associates Publishing.

Acrostic Tiering Chart

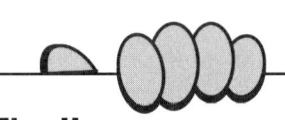

Tier I: Simpler Applications	Tier II: More Complex Applications
Students complete provided acrostic using the CD template or working on paper.	Students create and complete original acrostic using the CD template or working on paper.
Students respond in words or phrases.	Students respond in sentences.
The content or topic is simple.	The content or topic is more abstract or complex.
The vocabulary is accurate but basic.	The vocabulary is more complex and applies multi-syllable words that are topic specific.
The teacher facilitates or pairs of students work together to support students' success.	Individuals complete the acrostic.
	Individuals or pairs complete a continuous-text acrostic in sequence.
	Individuals or pairs of students plan a key concept word and develop an acrostic using beyond grade-level resources.

Kingore, B. (2008). *Teaching Without Nonsense*, 2nd ed. Austin, TX: Professional Associates Publishing.

Acrostic

TOPIC _____

RESOURCE(S) _____

_____

R _____

E _____

S _____

E _____

A _____

R _____

C _____

H _____

Kingore, B. (2008). *Teaching Without Nonsense*, 2nd ed. Austin, TX: Professional Associates Publishing.

Acrostic

TITLE _____

AUTHOR _____

G _____

R _____

E _____

A _____

T _____

B _____

O _____

O _____

K _____

SECTION 2: Learning Experiences

Analysis Grid

Grade Levels: K-12

K-1 with teacher facilitation; 2-12 in small groups or independently

An analysis grid learning experience:
- Categorizes and organizes information in a comparative form.
- Analyzes and compares the significant attributes of a topic.
- Serves as a springboard for discussing, researching, or writing more extensively about a topic.
- Enables teachers to preassess and evaluate students' accuracy, depth, and complexity of information.

An analysis grid is a graphic organizer for analyzing the attributes or major characteristics of a topic or subject (Pittelman, 1991). It activates students' schema about the topic and focuses their discussions and further learning. The categorization promotes students' long-term memory.

Model this learning task using a simple, well-known topic to teach the process. An example from a primary class analyzing mammals, fish, and crustaceans is shared here to illustrate one application. For the selected topic, list the subparts or examples on the left of the grid, and then list several attributes across the top to label each column. As a class, discuss the characteristics, and in each cell of the grid, place a plus sign (+) or Y (yes) if that attribute is valid; write a minus sign (-) or N (no) if the attribute is not applicable.

Analysis Grid
TOPIC: **Animals**
CODE: **Y=yes   N=no**

	omnivore	herbivore	carnivore	has gills	has lungs	swims	walks	lives on land	lives in water	lays eggs	live birth
Mammal	Y	Y	Y	N	Y	Y	Y	Y	Y	Y	Y
Fish	Y	Y	Y	Y	N	Y	N	N	Y	Y	N
Crustacean	Y	Y	Y	Y	N	Y	Y	Y	Y	Y	N

Kingore, B. (2008). *Teaching Without Nonsense*, 2nd ed. Austin, TX: Professional Associates Publishing.

Facilitate as the class works together to complete the grid, and then, discuss the similarities and differences observed on the completed grid. Challenge students to expand the grid with another attribute or another example to compare.

As a closure, the class concludes several comparative statements, such as *Mammals, fish, and crustaceans can all live in water.* Sincerely compliment strong ideas and discuss how the class used each of the following skills during this process.

- Analysis
- Compare and contrast
- Synthesis

Two included templates for analysis grids provide a simpler and more detailed version of the learning experience. Introduce the task using the simpler version. Continue using that version when it is appropriate to the topic depth or the age of the students. The second template allows a more complex and detailed analysis by providing extended areas to include attributes and subparts of the topic.

Analysis Grid

TOPIC: **Polygons**
CODE: **A=always   N=never   S=sometimes**

	Straight sides	Closed figure	Four sides	Angles are equal	Sides are equal length	Parallel sides	Symmetrical	Sum of angles = 180°	Sum of angles = 360°	FORMULA: Area = base x height
triangle	A	A	N	S	S	N	S	A	N	N
square	A	A	A	A	A	A	A	N	A	A
rectangle	A	A	A	A	N	A	A	N	A	A
pentagon	A	A	N	S	S	S	S	N	N	N
hexagon	A	A	N	S	S	S	S	N	N	N
octagon	A	A	N	S	S	S	S	N	N	N
parallelogram	A	A	A	S	S	A	A	N	A	A
quadrilateral	A	A	A	S	S	S	S	N	A	S

Content Applications

Language Arts
- Authors, characters, settings, genres, fiction, non-fiction, books about the same topic, or themes in multiple pieces of literature

Math
- Operations, geometric shapes, processes, or strategies

Science
- Environments, plants, diseases, cycles, space, body systems, or ocean life

Social Studies
- Cultures, pollution issues, conservation strategies, government organizations, political systems, states, countries, or human behaviors

Health and Physical Education
- Types of drugs and their effects, safety, or game rules and procedures

---

Kingore, B. (2008). *Teaching Without Nonsense*, 2nd ed. Austin, TX: Professional Associates Publishing.

Variations

- Use initial letters instead of a plus and minus sign as the rating in each cell. When a narrow range is more appropriate, as with young learners, use *Y* for yes and *N* for no. For a wider range of rating, possibilities include: *A = Always, F = Frequently, S = Sometimes,* and *N = Never.*

- Use a rating continuum of one to three or of one to five to mark in each cell. The continuum demonstrates the relative importance of each attribute. In general, the wider the continuum, the more complex the analysis and discussion. However, a wide continuum typically requires more time for students to complete because of the discussion and negotiation that is required to reach consensus.

- Initially, preselect the attributes for students to analyze. With experience, enhance high-level thinking and content mastery by challenging students to identify the attributes of the topic and determine which to list across the top of the grid. Have students work in small groups to determine attributes; then, meet as a whole class to compare, discuss, and reach consensus regarding the most significant attribute choices.

- Analysis grids enable students to identify and categorize information for comparative writing. Students use the grid as a tool to organize the comparison and contrast of information before beginning the writing task.

- Use an analysis grid to evaluate students' accuracy and depth of information. The grid serves as a test when students are required to individually complete a grid using the attributes and topic subparts listed on the grid. To increase the assessment challenge, preselect only the topic and subparts for the grid. Students are then evaluated on the quality and quantity of their decisions regarding the most significant attributes to include as well as their analysis ratings.

Options for Implementation

Pre- and Post-Assessment

As a preassessment of background knowledge and understanding when the class

Analysis Grid

TOPIC: Organelles
CODE: A=always S=sometimes
      N=never   ?=Don't know
September 9

	Nucleus	Chloroplast	Cell wall
Animalia	A	N	N
Fungi	A	?	A
Monera	A	?	S
Plantae	A	A	A
Protista	A	?	S

Kingore, B. (2008). *Teaching Without Nonsense*, 2nd ed. Austin, TX: Professional Associates Publishing.

begins a new topic, each student completes a grid by recording the date and ratings using a colored pen. Students review the results and set goals regarding the changes in their achievement that they intend to accomplish by the next assessment.

After instruction in that topic is complete, the students revisit their previous assessments and use a different color of ink to record the date and embellish, delete, or correct items on the preassessment. The use of a different color allows students to document progress by validating their increased accuracy, understanding, and quantity of information.

Comprehending Change Over Time

Draw a diagonal in each cell of the grid. Students complete the grid by recording responses in the top half of the grid at the beginning of their study and then revisit the grid to record responses in the bottom half of the grid at the conclusion of the segment of learning. For example, using a continuum of one to five, record public perspectives of issues at the beginning and

Analysis Grid

TOPIC Organelles
CODE A=always S=sometimes
     N=never   ?=Don't know

September 9/May 27

	Nucleus	Chloroplast	Cell wall	Mitochondria	Ribosome	Smooth Endoplasmic reticulum	Golgi apparatus	Vacuole	Plasma membrane	Rough Endoplasmic reticulum
Animalia	A	N	N	A	A	A	A	A	A	A
Fungi	A	N	A	A	A	A	A	N	A	A
Monera	N/A	S	S	N	A	N	N	N/A	A	N
Plantae	A	A	A	A	A	A	A	A	A	A
Protista	A	S	N/S	A	A	A	A	S	A	A

Analysis Grid

TOPIC **Sarah, Plain, and Tall by Patricia MacLachlan**
Beginning/end of book
Rating: 1-3 (3=high degree)

	happy	Hopeful	Angry	Confident	Lonely
Sarah	2	1	1	2	3
Jacob/Papa	2	2	1	2	3
Anna	2	1	3	2	3
Caleb	2	2	2	1	3

Analysis Grid

TOPIC **Sarah, Plain, and Tall by Patricia MacLachlan**
Beginning/end of book
Rating: 1-3 (3=high degree)

	happy	Hopeful	Angry	Confident	Lonely
Sarah	2 / 3	1 / 3	1 / 1	2 / 3	3 / 1
Jacob/Papa	2 / 3	2 / 3	1 / 1	2 / 2	3 / 1
Anna	2 / 3	1 / 3	3 / 1	2 / 2	3 / 1
Caleb	2 / 3	2 / 3	2 / 1	1 / 3	3 / 1

Kingore, B. (2008). *Teaching Without Nonsense*, 2nd ed. Austin, TX: Professional Associates Publishing.

SECTION 2: Learning Experiences

Analysis Grid

TOPIC: Holes by Louis Sachar
CODE: 1=lowest   5=highest
Beginning of the book / End of the book

	Naive	Smart	Hopeful	Persistent	Lucky	Angry	Confident	Happy	Caring	Successful
Stanley	4/2	2/4	2/5	3/5	1/5	3/1	1/4	2/4	4/4	1/5
Father	3/3	4/4	4/4	5/5	1/5	1/1	3/3	2/5	3/4	1/5
Zero	2/2	2/5	1/5	2/5	1/5	4/1	1/4	1/5	2/4	1/5
Warden	1/1	4/4	4/1	5/5	1/1	5/5	5/1	3/1	1/1	3/1

Analysis Grid

TOPIC: English punctuation errors
CODE: A=always   N=never   S=sometimes
Find ten errors in this punctuation grid.

	Ends a sentence	Begins a sentence	In the middle of a sentence	Used in bibliographies	Used in a number	Used with people's names	Used in addresses	Used in quotations	Used in abbreviations
.	A	N	N	A	S	S	S	S	A
,	N	N	S	A	S	N	S	S	N
-	N	N	S	S	S	S	N	S	N
!	S	N	N	N	N	N	N	S	N
?	S	N	N	S	N	N	N	S	N
" "	S	S	S	N	N	N	N	A	N
( )	S	S	S	A	N	S	N	N	N
…	S	N	S	S	N	N	N	S	N

Analysis Grid

TOPIC: English punctuation errors
CODE: A=always   N=never   S=sometimes
Find ten errors in this punctuation grid.

	Ends a sentence	Begins a sentence	In the middle of a sentence	Used in bibliographies	Used in a number	Used with people's names	Used in addresses	Used in quotations	Used in abbreviations
.	**S**	N	**S**	A	S	S	S	**S**	
,	N	N	S	A	S	**S**	S	S	N
-	N	N	S	S	S	S	**S**	S	N
!	S	N	**S**	**S**	N	N	N	S	N
?	S	N	**S**	S	N	N	N	S	N
" "	S	S	S	N	N	N	N	A	N
( )	S	S	S	A	N	S	N	**S**	N
…	S	**S**	S	S	N	N	N	S	N

Kingore, B. (2008). *Teaching Without Nonsense*, 2nd ed. Austin, TX: Professional Associates Publishing.

---

then at the end of a historical war or conflict. Examples shared here illustrate how students interpret the change within characters in a novel after reading the first chapter or so and then after completing the book.

Error Analysis

Provide students with copies of a completed Analysis Grid for a current topic or skill. Purposely prepare the grid with multiple errors. As a closure task, inform the class that there are errors in the responses. Decide whether or not to tell them the total number of errors. Challenge students to work in pairs or trios for a few minutes to see how many of the errors they can identify and explain how to correct. Many students respond enthusiastically to the novelty of finding others' errors. The included example of English punctuation errors is an example of using an analysis grid with errors to promote discussion and integration of skills.

Analysis Grid Tiering Chart

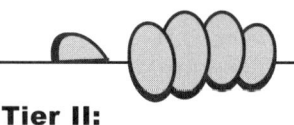

Tier I: Simpler Applications	Tier II: More Complex Applications
With adult support, students complete an analytical grid using the CD template or working on a paper copy.	Without adult assistance, students complete a more complex analytical grid using the CD template or working on a paper copy.
Students use the shorter form.	Students complete the longer form.
Students complete the task in small groups.	Students work individually to complete the task.
The content or topic is simple.	The content or topic is more abstract or complex.
The attributes are appropriate but basic.	The attributes are more specific, complex, or sophisticated.
Students encode the form using a narrow range, such as two or three variables or a one-to-three continuum.	Students encode the form using a wider range of variables or a one-to-five continuum.
The teacher structures all subparts and attributes for students to analyze.	A small group or an individual structures additional attributes to analyze.
The teacher structures subparts, some attributes, and facilitates as students determine additional attributes to analyze.	A small group or an individual structures additional subparts and attributes.
	An individual or small group uses the CD template or paper copy to structure and complete an analysis grid for an assigned or individually researched topic.

Kingore, B. (2008). *Teaching Without Nonsense*, 2nd ed. Austin, TX: Professional Associates Publishing.

Analysis Grid

TOPIC _____

CODE _____

Analysis Grid

TOPIC _____

CODE _____

Kingore, B. (2008). *Teaching Without Nonsense*, 2nd ed. Austin, TX: Professional Associates Publishing.

Body Rhymes

Grade Levels: Primary

The body rhymes learning experience:
- Actively engages students in whole body responses involving rhyming, body parts, auditory discrimination, listening, and following directions.
- Appeals to visual, oral/auditory, and kinesthetic learners.
- Integrates reading and writing skills.
- Encourages children's high-level thinking and flexible thinking.
- Assesses vocabulary and fluency in English or other languages.

Body rhymes are simple rhyming couplets for different parts of the body. Understanding words for body parts is an important vocabulary task as well as being so directly correlated to mental development that it is often a component of intelligence and achievement tests. The rhyming aspect is significant as many children come to school today without background opportunities in the rhyme and phonemic discrimination that relates to literacy development.

Model this task by brainstorming with the children the various parts of the body that are important for children to know. Prompt their responses by asking:

> • *What parts of your body can you see outside of your clothes?*

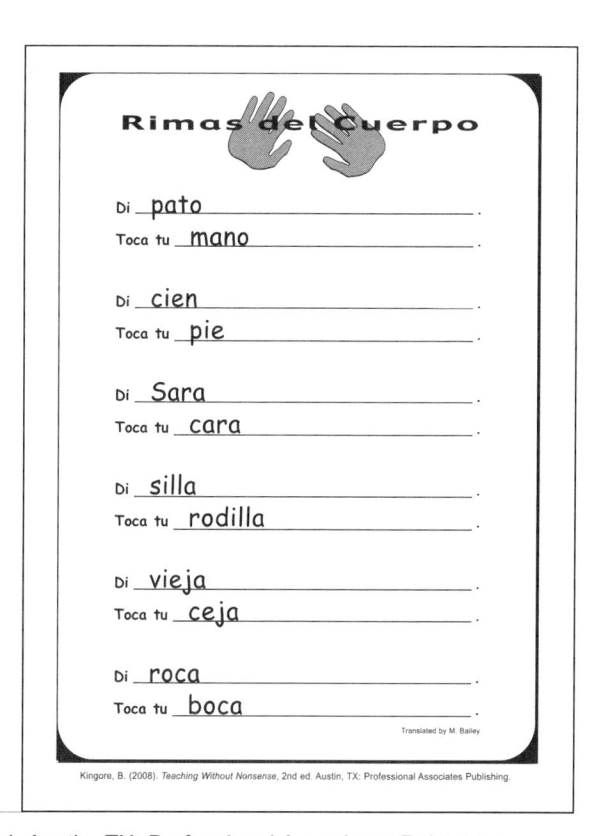

Rimas del Cuerpo

Di _pato_.
Toca tu _mano_.

Di _cien_.
Toca tu _pie_.

Di _Sara_.
Toca tu _cara_.

Di _silla_.
Toca tu _rodilla_.

Di _vieja_.
Toca tu _ceja_.

Di _roca_.
Toca tu _boca_.

Translated by M. Bailey

Kingore, B. (2008). *Teaching Without Nonsense*, 2nd ed. Austin, TX: Professional Associates Publishing.

Kingore, B. (2008). *Teaching Without Nonsense*, 2nd ed. Austin, TX: Professional Associates Publishing.

- *What parts would you find inside your shoes?*
- *What parts would you find inside a glove?*

List their ideas on the chalkboard or a chart. Then, have a child select one of the body parts and guide the class to brainstorm together two or three rhyming words for that body part. List those words beside the name of the body part. This listing provides an effective time to accent phonemes and point out to the children that all rhyming words do not use the same spelling pattern. In some classes, teachers categorize the children's rhyming as words and non-words to facilitate children's developing awareness of those differences.

On a chart, chalkboard, or overhead, display the rhyme pattern provided in this section. Demonstrate how to record the rhyming word on the first line and the body part on the second line to complete a body rhyme chant. Have the children repeat the rhyme as they perform the suggested movement. Later, have them perform the same rhyme again, but touch the part of the body in a different way to promote flexible thinking and fluency.

Continue the process with another body part and create multiple verses. As children's interests dictate, complete two or more rhymes at one time. Then, return to the task another time to add more rhymes. Eventually, most classes create and can read and perform multiple verses of body rhymes. Children are motivated to repeat the rhymes multiple times during stretch breaks and transitions. Their rhymes may be similar to these:

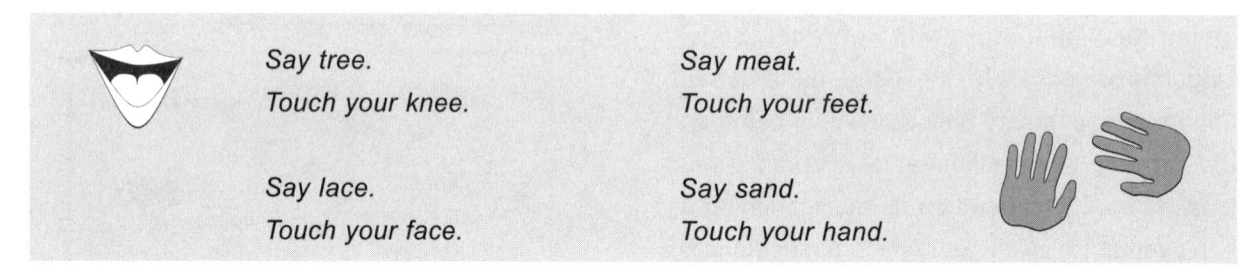

Say tree.
Touch your knee.

Say lace.
Touch your face.

Say meat.
Touch your feet.

Say sand.
Touch your hand.

Variations

- When appropriate, encourage individual children to create new rhymes. Have each child write and illustrate a rhyme to combine into a class book or an individual collection.

- This activity adapts well to multiple languages by using body parts and rhyming words in a language other than English. As a comparative thinking task, challenge children to complete the learning experience in more than one language.

- As appropriate, increase the challenge by having children add descriptions, directions, and elaborations to the rhymes they create. Children writing the rhymes can also be guided to apply appropriate writing conventions, such as capitol letters and punctuation.

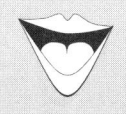

> *Say fire alarm.*
> *Touch your right arm.*
>
> *Say apple pie.*
> *Touch your left eye.*
>
> *Say red rose.*
> *Touch your funny nose.*

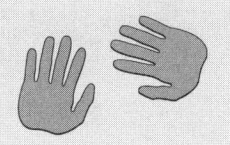

- Greater skill is required when using two-syllable words that name body parts because of the increased difficulty presented by two-syllable rhymes. Some children enjoy the challenge of creating body rhymes with two-syllable words.

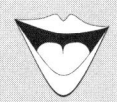

> *Say "Don't linger!"*
> *Touch your little finger.*
>
> *Say work folder.*
> *Touch your neighbor's shoulder.*

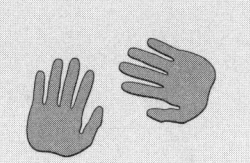

Options for Implementation

One a Day

Use body rhymes as a continuing feature and daily opening or closure technique. The class works together to create one new rhyme to add to the class chart each day. Then, everyone stands and performs the rhymes together. Allow different children to use a pointer to track the print as the class performs.

Kingore, B. (2008). *Teaching Without Nonsense*, 2nd ed. Austin, TX: Professional Associates Publishing.

Body Rhymes Tiering Chart

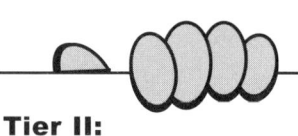

Tier I: Simpler Applications	Tier II: More Complex Applications
The activity is completed as a teacher-directed, whole-class task.	With adult support, individuals orally create rhymes.
Teacher scribes the children's ideas using the CD template or a paper copy.	Individuals create and write rhymes using the CD template or a paper copy.
The class or small groups read the chants together.	Individuals fluently read and expand the chants.
The vocabulary is accurate but basic.	The vocabulary is more descriptive and applies multi-syllable words.
The rhyme uses one-syllable words for body parts.	The rhyme uses two-syllable words for body parts.
	Individuals or pairs of students work together to complete rhymes in more than one language.

Kingore, B. (2008). *Teaching Without Nonsense*, 2nd ed. Austin, TX: Professional Associates Publishing.

Body Rhymes

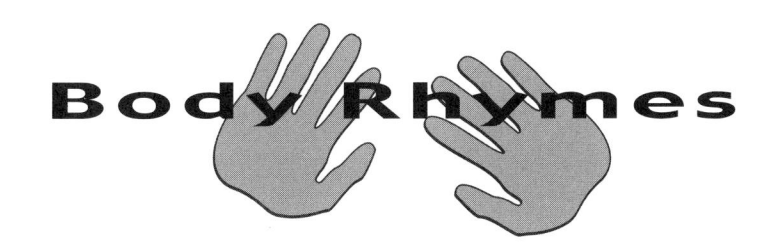

Say _____.

Touch your _____.

Say _____.

Touch your _____.

Say _____.

Touch your _____.

Say _____.

Touch your _____.

Say _____.

Touch your _____.

Say _____.

Touch your _____.

Kingore, B. (2008). *Teaching Without Nonsense*, 2nd ed. Austin, TX: Professional Associates Publishing.

Rimas del Cuerpo

Di _____ .

Toca tu _____ .

Di _____ .

Toca tu _____ .

Di _____ .

Toca tu _____ .

Di _____ .

Toca tu _____ .

Di _____ .

Toca tu _____ .

Di _____ .

Toca tu _____ .

Translated by M. Bailey

SECTION 2: Learning Experiences

Comic Character

Grade Levels: 2 - 12

The comic character learning experience:
- Actively engages students in quick sketches and art responses.
- Engages visual, spatial, and kinesthetic learners in logical thinking.
- Reviews and synthesizes information.
- Relates the work being studied to students' lives and experiences.
- Revitalizes and mentally engages students through a fast-paced response.

Art adds a rich dimension to learning. Integrating opportunities for quick sketching increases vocabulary development and allows students to benefit from this visual pathway to memory and long-term learning (ASCD. 2006; Willis, 2006).

Many students like to draw comic figures. Connect that enjoyment with content by inviting students to quickly sketch original comic characters and draw a speech balloon or conversation bubble by the character. Students then integrate the content being studied by writing a content-related response in the speech balloon.

The comic character activity is most effective when completed as a fast-paced, energized response. Allow only a brief time, such as two or three minutes, for students to complete a drawing. When students do not believe they can draw well enough, encourage them to get ideas or visually select examples from the graphics on the Comic Characters page to combine and create a character's face.

Kingore, B. (2008). *Teaching Without Nonsense*, 2nd ed. Austin, TX: Professional Associates Publishing.

Consider the following sequence to model this learning experience.

1. Make an overhead transparency of the comic character page. Use a piece of card stock or construction paper to cover the comic transparency on the overhead and show the students only the title of the page.
2. Announce that they are each going to draw an original comic character that has never been seen before and that they are going to complete their drawing in two minutes or less. Then, move the card stock or construction paper down to reveal one line at a time.
3. As students view a row of sketches, ask them to draw a head using one of these ideas or a better one of their own. Then, ask them to add some hair and so on as each row of sketches is revealed.
4. For the final row, ask students to select details to add to customize their drawing and elaborate their own ideas.
5. When the two minutes of sketching time are done, invite students to share their drawing with each other and talk about the process.
6. Finally, ask students to draw a conversation bubble and write one thing they feel or think about doing this drawing.

This activity is an effective way to review key points and reach closure for a lesson or discussion. The following are examples of sentence stems that might be used to prompt students' content responses to incorporate with their quick-sketch comic character.

- *The most important point is _____.*
- *I want to remember _____.*
- *This reminds me _____.*
- *This is similar to _____.*
- *I believe that _____.*
- *What should happen next is _____.*
- *An essential question is _____.*
- *The best way to do this is _____.*
- *The main idea is _____.*
- *The three most important words about this topic are _____.*

Enhance the effectiveness of the activity by asking students to share and compare their responses with one another. Briefly discussing these ideas is another factor in assisting memory and achievement.

CAUTION: Avoid providing students with a copy of the comic characters. Teachers found that students were inclined to trace the parts rather than exert any attempt to draw when a copy was available. Post the comic characters for visual viewing and analysis, but not where students can trace them.

Kingore, B. (2008). *Teaching Without Nonsense*, 2nd ed. Austin, TX: Professional Associates Publishing.

Variations

- For increased high-level thinking, use the students' responses to promote consensus building. In small groups of two or three, students discuss individual responses and agree upon their best ideas. The groups then share their results with the entire class. The critical analysis and negotiations that ensue further serve to help students integrate information about the topic.

- Challenge students to complete the talk balloon from another's perspective. How would the antagonist respond? What might the defeated group want us to understand?

- Encourage students to develop a comic strip that has characters talking about and explaining the topic under study.

- Promote more creativity and original art by involving students in developing a class version of a comic character chart. Display the comic character chart that provides only one example sketch in each row. Invite students to express their ideas by drawing new sketch examples in any row. Place the chart in easy access so students can cooperatively work on it over several days. When each row of the chart is full, use the class chart for comic character learning experience applications.

Options for Implementation

Journal Writing

To revive interest in journal writing and lab reports, have students draw a character at the bottom corner of the page. Then, they add a large conversation bubble that covers the rest of the page and write their journal or lab response in that bubble.

Kingore, B. (2008). *Teaching Without Nonsense*, 2nd ed. Austin, TX: Professional Associates Publishing.

Comic Characters Tiering Chart

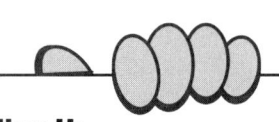

Tier I: Simpler Applications	Tier II: More Complex Applications
Students are guided by the teacher to complete a comic character on paper.	Students complete a more complex, detailed comic character on paper.
As needed, students work in pairs to complete the content response and support each others' success.	Students individually complete a content response featuring complex, detailed information.
The content or topic is simple.	The content or topic is more abstract or complex.
Students express an accurate content response in words or phrases.	Students respond in content-rich sentences that demonstrate abstract thinking, multiple perspectives, and issues.
The response incorporates accurate but basic vocabulary.	The response incorporates more complex vocabulary and applies multi-syllable words that are topic specific.
	Students use the draw feature of a computer to develop original sketches as options to create additional comic characters.

Kingore, B. (2008). *Teaching Without Nonsense*, 2nd ed. Austin, TX: Professional Associates Publishing.

SECTION 2: Learning Experiences

Comic Characters

| HEADS |
| HAIR |
| EYES |
| NOSES |
| MOUTHS |
| EARS |
| DETAILS |

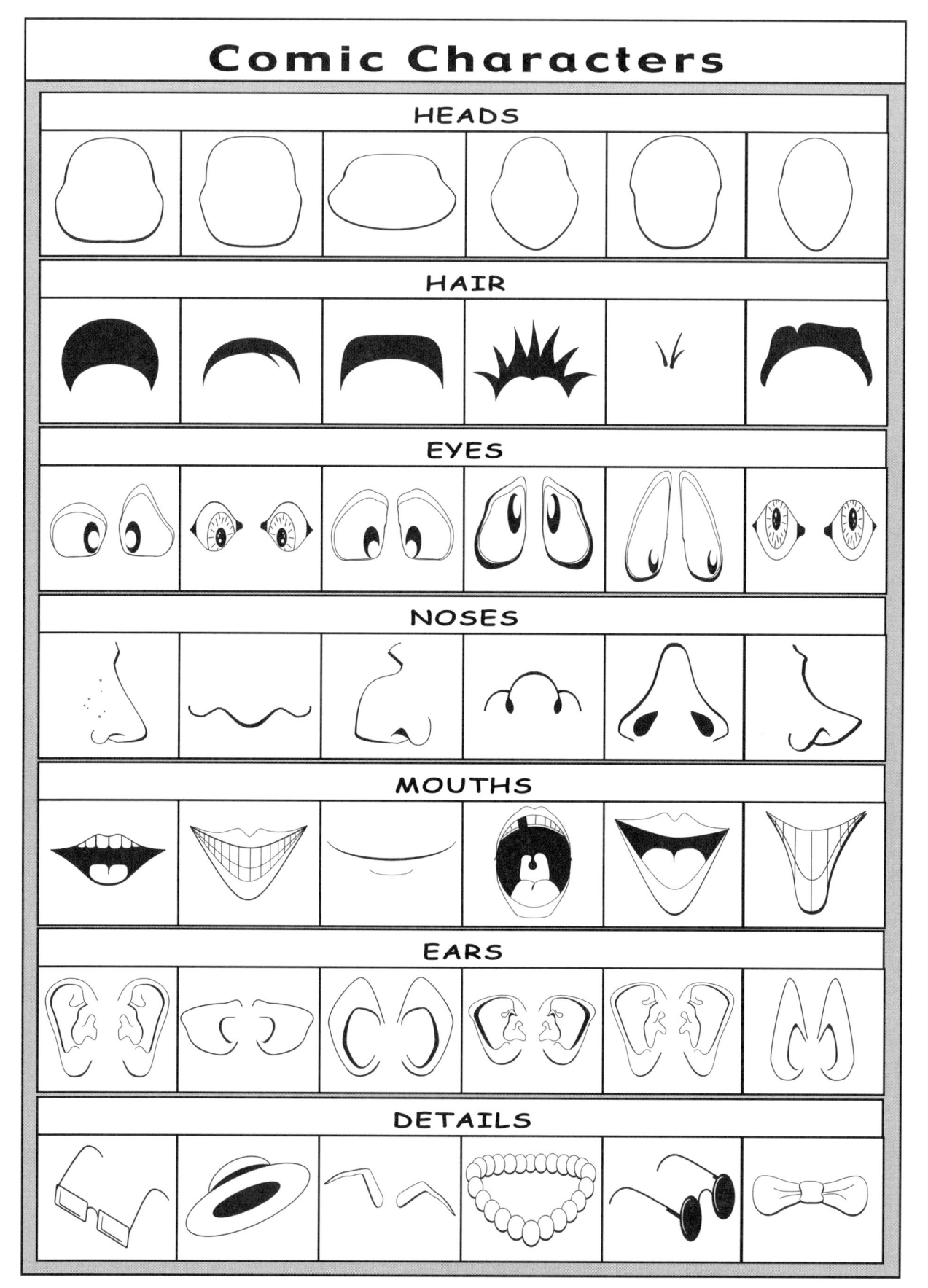

Kingore, B. (2008). *Teaching Without Nonsense*, 2nd ed. Austin, TX: Professional Associates Publishing.

Personajes ChistOsos

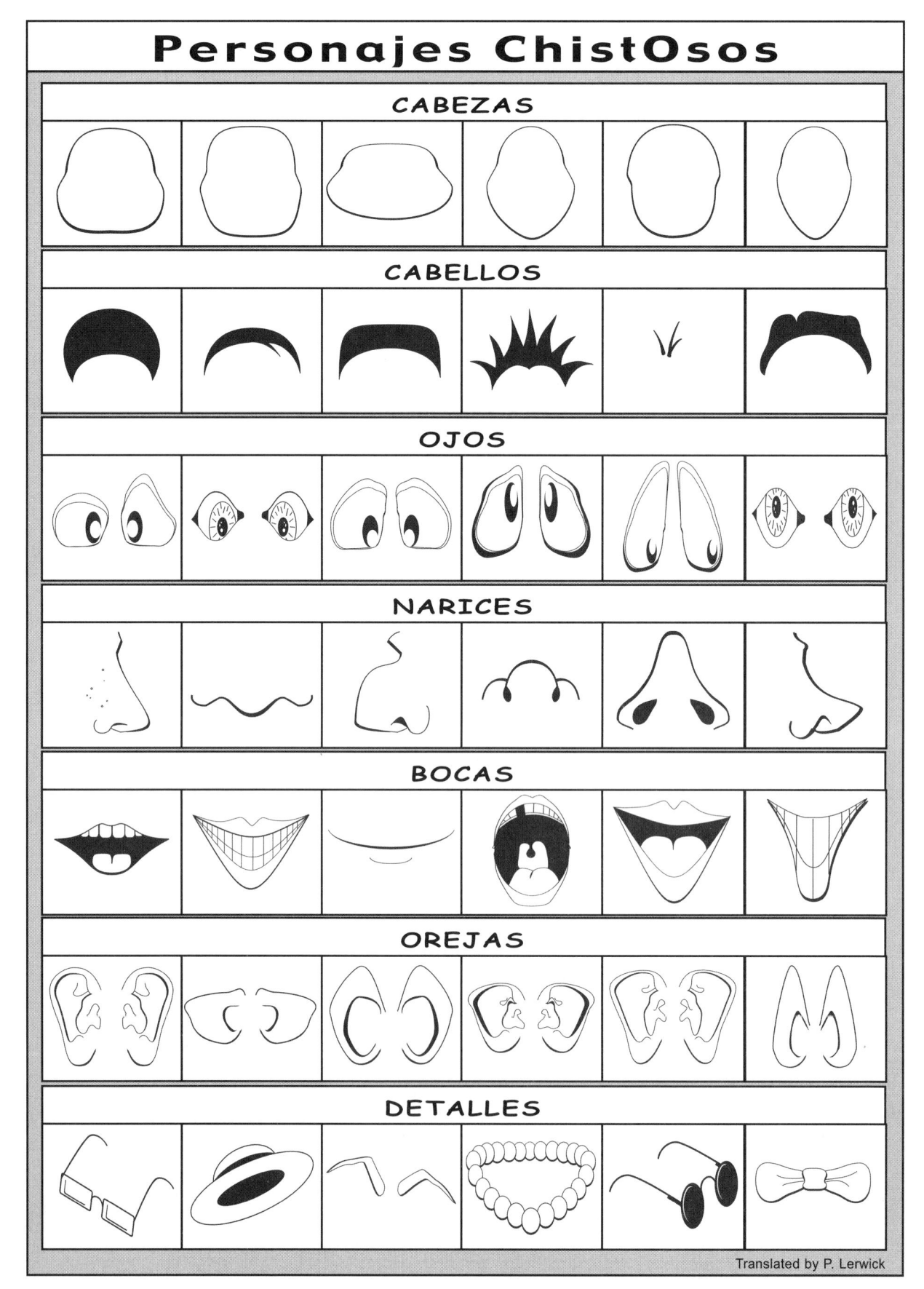

CABEZAS

CABELLOS

OJOS

NARICES

BOCAS

OREJAS

DETALLES

Translated by P. Lerwick

Kingore, B. (2008). *Teaching Without Nonsense*, 2nd ed. Austin, TX: Professional Associates Publishing.

Comic Characters

	HEADS					

	HAIR					

	EYES					

	NOSES					

	MOUTHS					

	EARS					

	DETAILS					

Kingore, B. (2008). *Teaching Without Nonsense*, 2nd ed. Austin, TX: Professional Associates Publishing.

Concept Map

Grade Levels: K-12

Kindergartners and first grade children complete this task with adult facilitation.

A concept map learning experience:
- Actively engages students in developing graphic responses.
- Enables students to visually represent the relationships within a topic, story, or concept, appealing to visual and spatial learners.
- Provides a simple-to-prepare-and-implement activity that connects to a myriad of topics, content areas, and skills.
- Promotes conceptual thinking more than recall or simple thinking.
- Serves as an assessment tool to assess the accuracy, depth, and complexity of information.

Concepts maps are graphic organizers that are used to structure topical information and relationships. These visual tools are referred to by several different names, including webs, mind maps, story maps, thinking maps, and semantic maps. They vary from simple to quite complex and are appropriate for any content area and grade level.

Since concept maps not only illustrate the depth of information but also the relationship of the ideas, concepts, and vocabulary under consideration, they are particularly effective when used as a pre- and post-assessment tool. Students complete a graphic

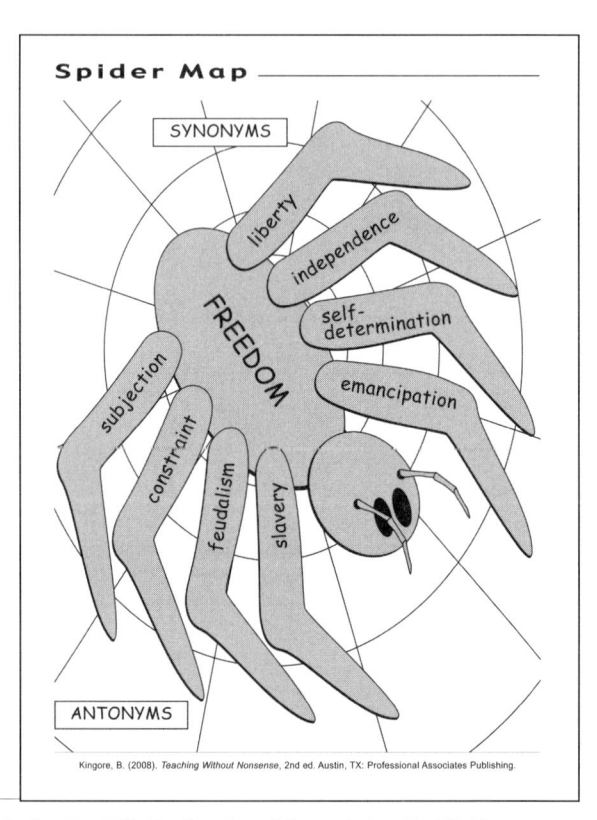

Spider Map

SYNONYMS: liberty, independence, self-determination, emancipation

FREEDOM

ANTONYMS: subjection, constraint, feudalism, slavery

Kingore, B. (2008). *Teaching Without Nonsense*, 2nd ed. Austin, TX: Professional Associates Publishing.

Kingore, B. (2008). *Teaching Without Nonsense*, 2nd ed. Austin, TX: Professional Associates Publishing.

when a segment of learning is initiated, and then, at the end of the unit, revisit the same graphic with a different colored pen to embellish what has been learned. and document continuous progress. This application enables children and families to compare how children's knowledge about the topic increases through their efforts and learning experiences.

Model this learning experience using a simple concept map and a high-interest topic. Since many students are familiar with this popular graphic tool, only brief instruction in the process may be needed.

1. Fold a piece of chart paper into quadrants and draw an oval in the center where the boxes intersect.
2. In the oval, write a concept or topic, such as pets. Label a category in each quadrant, such as types, attributes, environments, and habits.
3. As a class or small group, brainstorm together to generate words and pictures to organize in each box to designate what is known about each category. Encourage children to use specific terms and more in-depth information.
4. As closure for the learning experience, guide the students to review the information and formulate a conclusion.

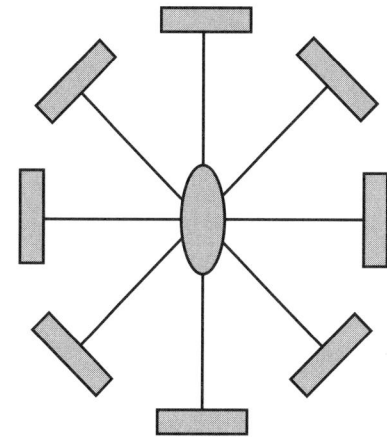

Information Patterns

Concept maps can be constructed in four basic patterns that organize information: conceptual, hierarchical, sequential, and cyclical (Bromley, Irwin De Vitis, & Modlo, 1995). The conceptual pattern begins with a central idea or category and is then surrounded by related or supporting information. Simple shapes, such as the spider and the hand, visually appeal to students and motivate them to organize information. The provided rectangle form invites more complex and elaborate responses. On this map, the center might include the theme, title of a book, or any concept being studied. The next sized shapes relate the key events, elements, or subconcepts. The smallest shapes contain the supporting details or examples.

Conceptual map

Hierarchical map

The hierarchical pattern ranks the details or subconcepts under the main concept. Science classifications, social systems, and the main idea-events-details of a story are effectively related in a hierarchical pattern.

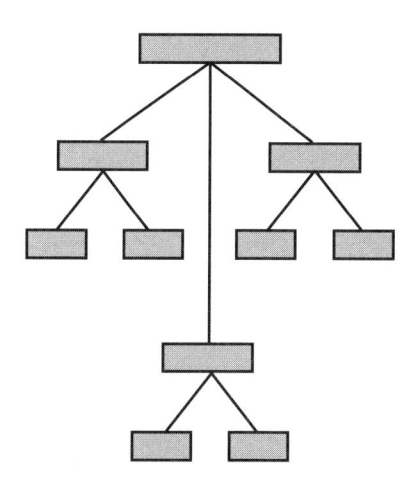

Kingore, B. (2008). *Teaching Without Nonsense*, 2nd ed. Austin, TX: Professional Associates Publishing.

The sequential pattern arranges information in a prescribed order such as a time line or a cause-effect diagram. One unusual example of this organization is a paper chain students construct that relates events in sequence or the steps in a process or experiment. Using cut paper strips, students write information on each strip that will be a link of the chain and then glue the chain together in sequence. The paper-chain concept map particularly appeals to kinesthetic learners who benefit from the hands-on, three-dimensional application.

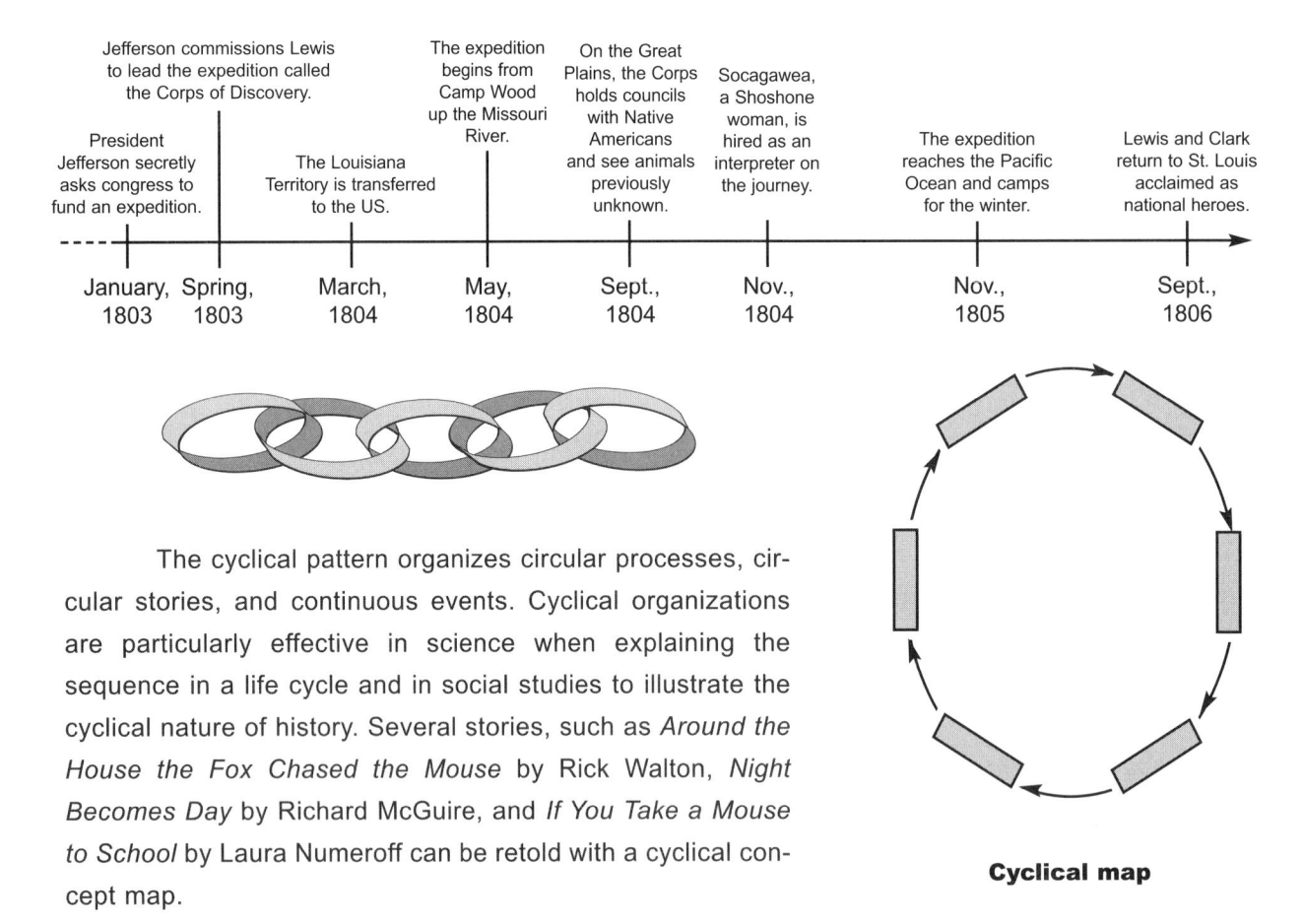

January, 1803	President Jefferson secretly asks congress to fund an expedition.
Spring, 1803	Jefferson commissions Lewis to lead the expedition called the Corps of Discovery.
March, 1804	The Louisiana Territory is transferred to the US.
May, 1804	The expedition begins from Camp Wood up the Missouri River.
Sept., 1804	On the Great Plains, the Corps holds councils with Native Americans and see animals previously unknown.
Nov., 1804	Socagawea, a Shoshone woman, is hired as an interpreter on the journey.
Nov., 1805	The expedition reaches the Pacific Ocean and camps for the winter.
Sept., 1806	Lewis and Clark return to St. Louis acclaimed as national heroes.

The cyclical pattern organizes circular processes, circular stories, and continuous events. Cyclical organizations are particularly effective in science when explaining the sequence in a life cycle and in social studies to illustrate the cyclical nature of history. Several stories, such as *Around the House the Fox Chased the Mouse* by Rick Walton, *Night Becomes Day* by Richard McGuire, and *If You Take a Mouse to School* by Laura Numeroff can be retold with a cyclical concept map.

Cyclical map

Combinations of these information patterns invite more in-depth and complex data while challenging high-level thinking. The place, event, and person forms shared in this section combine elements of the conceptual, hierarchal, and sequential patterns. Tier II of the event and person maps extend the required depth of information and are effective products to relate the biographical and topical research students complete.

Variations

- Vary the hand graphic by adding investigative words, such as who what, where, when, and why, or who, what, where, cause, and effect. Students use the handy organizer to relate a historical

Kingore, B. (2008). *Teaching Without Nonsense*, 2nd ed. Austin, TX: Professional Associates Publishing.

SECTION 2: Learning Experiences

event, a personal experience, or an event in a story. This variation is an effective tool that students can use to generate and organize information as a plan before completing a longer written discourse, as in this fifth grader's plan for a story shown here.

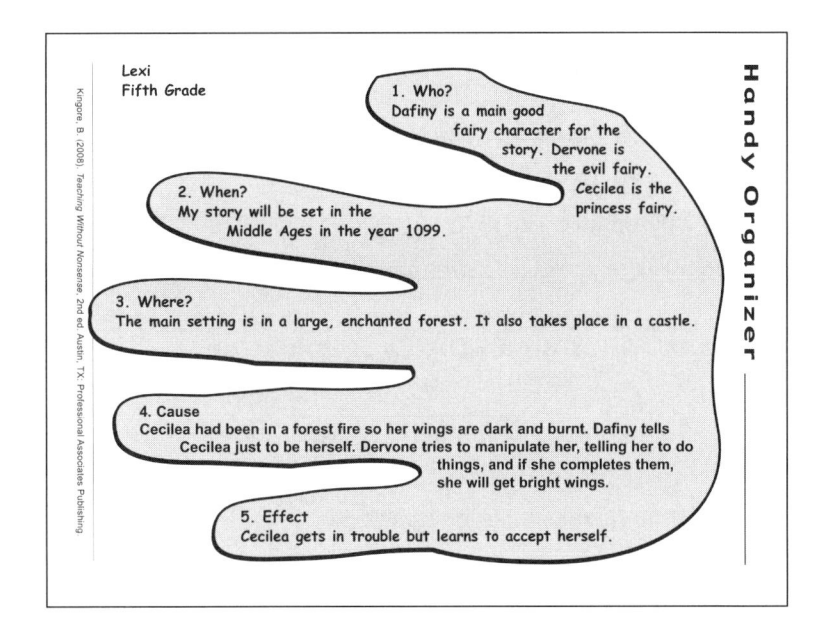

Handy Organizer

Lexi
Fifth Grade

1. Who?
Dafiny is a main good fairy character for the story. Dervone is the evil fairy. Cecilea is the princess fairy.

2. When?
My story will be set in the Middle Ages in the year 1099.

3. Where?
The main setting is in a large, enchanted forest. It also takes place in a castle.

4. Cause
Cecilea had been in a forest fire so her wings are dark and burnt. Dafiny tells Cecilea just to be herself. Dervone tries to manipulate her, telling her to do things, and if she completes them, she will get bright wings.

5. Effect
Cecilea gets in trouble but learns to accept herself.

- Use the rectangle map to visually model a topic outline. With the class, complete a rectangle map for a topic. Then, refer to one of the larger rectangles and its three connected smaller rectangles to write the outline of a paragraph with a topic sentence and details. Ask students to continue completing the topic outline. Some visual students benefit from developing a rectangle map as a planning outline before they write longer discourse.

- Challenge students to use two copies of the same concept map and complete each from a different perspective, such as opposing view points in an issue or two characters in a story.

- Invite students to draw additional areas on any concept map to expand places for more details and examples.

- Use an internet search engine to seek different examples of graphics for concept maps. Many sites are free and suitable for student applications.

- Invite visual-spatial students to create original concept map forms that they or other students use to communicate content relationships.

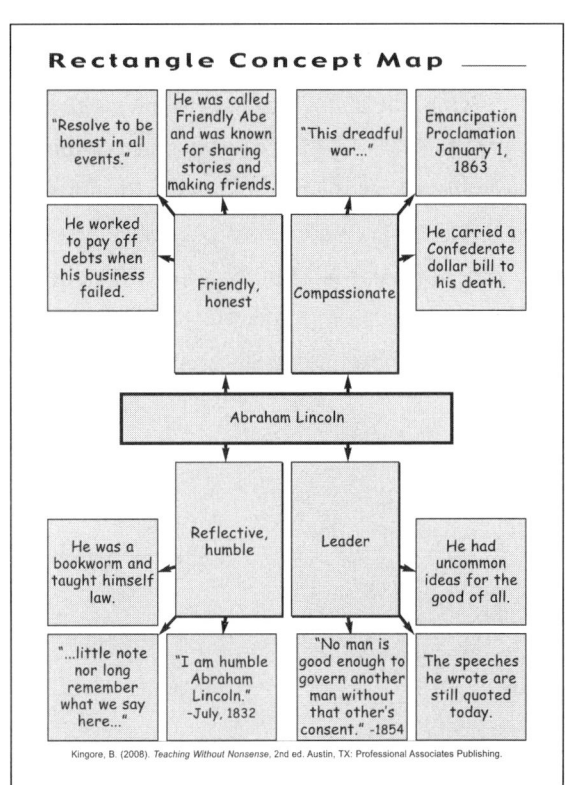

Rectangle Concept Map

"Resolve to be honest in all events."

He was called Friendly Abe and was known for sharing stories and making friends.

"This dreadful war..."

Emancipation Proclamation January 1, 1863

He worked to pay off debts when his business failed.

Friendly, honest

Compassionate

He carried a Confederate dollar bill to his death.

Abraham Lincoln

He was a bookworm and taught himself law.

Reflective, humble

Leader

He had uncommon ideas for the good of all.

"...little note nor long remember what we say here..."

"I am humble Abraham Lincoln." -July, 1832

"No man is good enough to govern another man without that other's consent." -1854

The speeches he wrote are still quoted today.

Kingore, B. (2008). *Teaching Without Nonsense*, 2nd ed. Austin, TX: Professional Associates Publishing.

Kingore, B. (2008). *Teaching Without Nonsense*, 2nd ed. Austin, TX: Professional Associates Publishing.

Options for Implementation

Enlarge the Concept Map

Enlarge the size of the graphic templates to provide a larger space for students able to embellish with extensive detail or to benefit students whose fine-motor capabilities require more room for writing.

Laminate for a Small-Group Application

Enlarge and laminate six to eight copies of a concept map. These tools can be repeatedly used by small groups to analyze the same topic and then compare their perspectives and information before forming class-wide conclusions.

Modeling for Depth and Complexity

Help students understand what depth and complexity of information look and sound like. To model the desired level of depth and complexity, partially complete a simple and more complex version of the same concept map before introducing the product to students. Elicit from the students the differences between simpler and more complex responses. Then, facilitate as students work together to construct in-depth and complex information to complete the graphic. Emphasize the difference between merely listing facts versus analyzing and organizing concepts and relationships.

Small-Group Cooperative Task

Using multiple copies of the same graphic, groups of two or three students work together to comprehend provided materials and complete a concept map for the targeted topic. The groups then come together as a whole class to share their information, discuss the content, and compare and contrast the differences in their products. The spirit of the exchange is information-sharing rather than only judging what is right or wrong. Emphasize the different perspectives, specific terminology, and depth of information; highlight the different ways groups organized accurate information. In this manner, concept maps serve as an excellent review and comparative thinking technique.

Kingore, B. (2008). *Teaching Without Nonsense*, 2nd ed. Austin, TX: Professional Associates Publishing.

Concept Map Tiering Chart

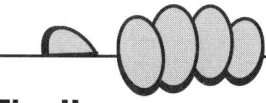

Tier I: Simpler Applications	Tier II: More Complex Applications
With adult support, students complete a concept map using the CD template or working on a paper copy.	Students complete a more complex concept map using the CD template or working on a paper copy.
The graphic requires brief and simple content.	The content, topic, and graphics are more elaborative, abstract, or complex.
Adults facilitate as students complete the task in small groups to support learning success.	Students complete the task in small groups to increase complexity and prompt diverse perspectives.
The provided resources are at grade level. The information included is appropriate but basic.	The provided resources are complex with beyond grade-level information.
The response uses words and phrases that are accurate but basic.	The response is written in sentences using multi-syllable, topic-specific words.
Some individuals are able to use the drawing feature of a computer to produce and complete a different version of a simple concept map.	Individually or in pairs, students use a computer to produce and complete a complex, multi-faceted version of a concept map to respond to an assigned or individually-researched topic.
	An individual creates a concept map using symbols requiring abstract thinking, different sizes of shapes to indicate the significance of ideas, and lines to establish sequence and relationships.

Kingore, B. (2008). *Teaching Without Nonsense*, 2nd ed. Austin, TX: Professional Associates Publishing.

Handy Organizer _____

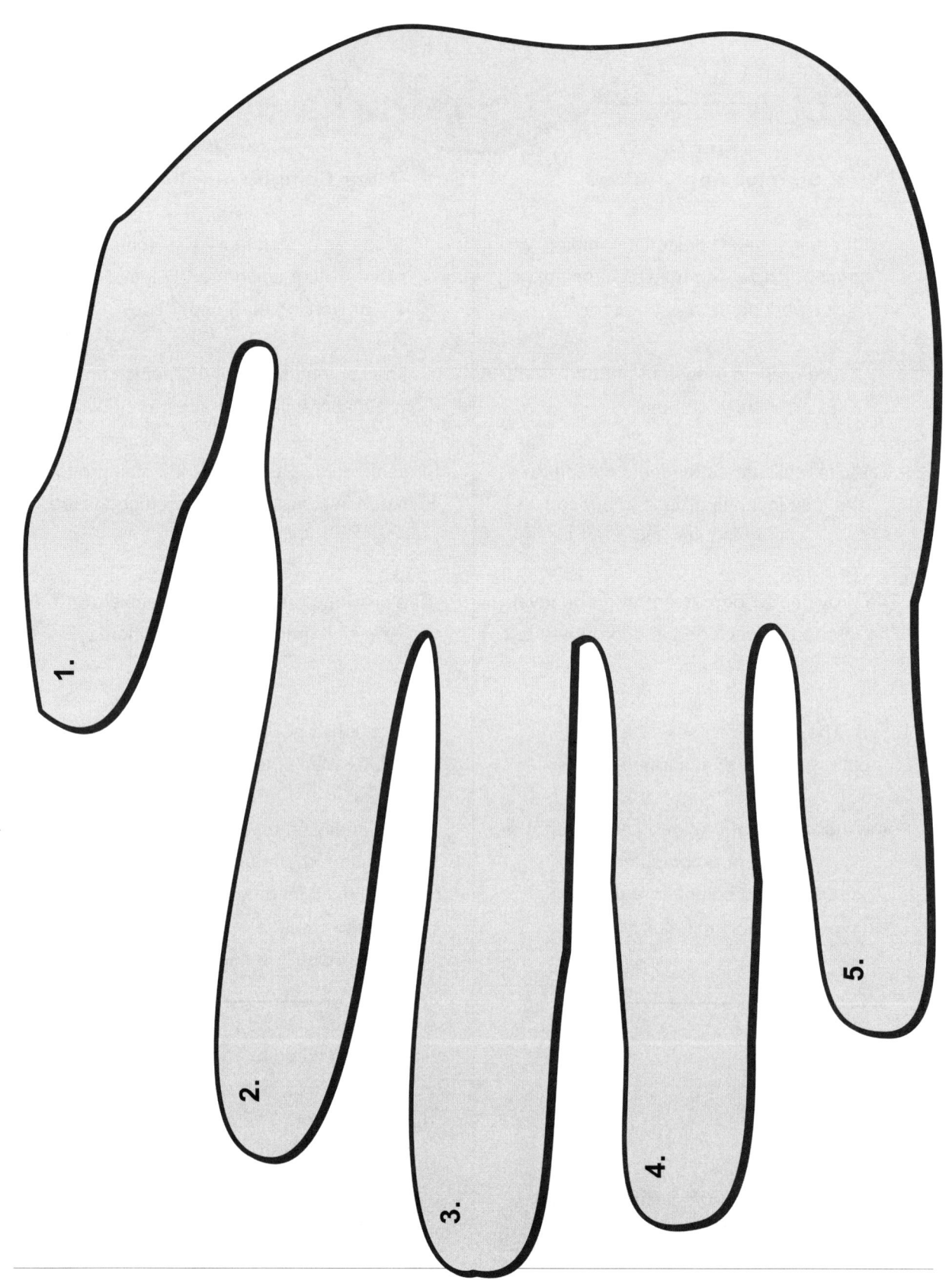

1.
2.
3.
4.
5.

Kingore, B. (2008). *Teaching Without Nonsense*, 2nd ed. Austin, TX: Professional Associates Publishing.

SECTION 2: Learning Experiences

Spider Map ──────────

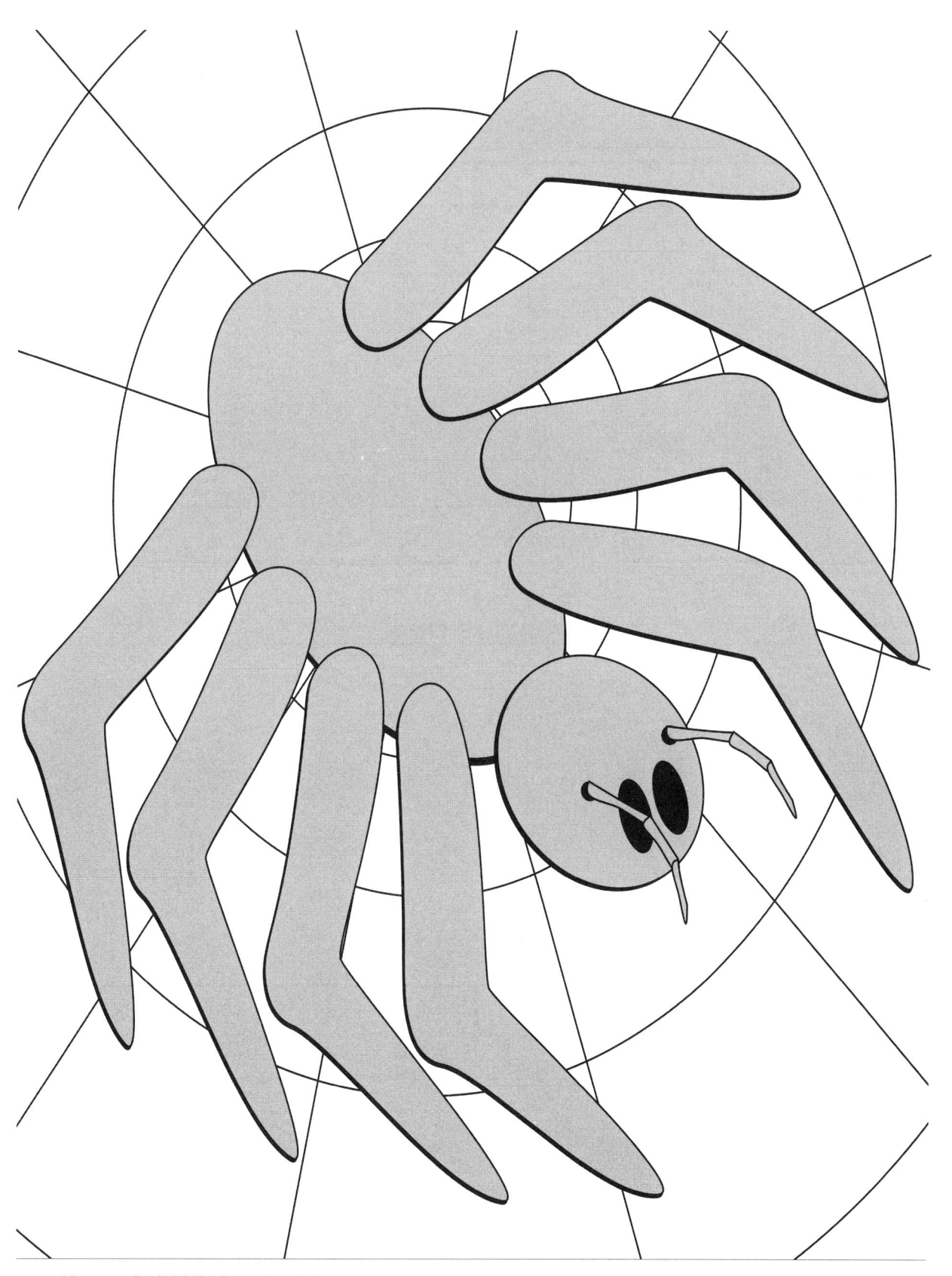

Kingore, B. (2008). *Teaching Without Nonsense*, 2nd ed. Austin, TX: Professional Associates Publishing.

Event Map:
Tier I

On the back, record the resources you used. Then, use sentences and/or symbols to complete the map.

MAIN EVENT:

PARTICIPANTS:

SETTING AND ISSUE:

WHAT HAPPENED:

EFFECTS:

Kingore, B. (2008). *Teaching Without Nonsense*, 2nd ed. Austin, TX: Professional Associates Publishing.

Mapa del Evento: Nivel I

En la parte de atrás, apunta los recursos o materiales que usaste. Después, utiliza oraciones o símbolos para terminar tu mapa.

EVENTO PRINCIPAL:

PARTICIPANTES:

LUGAR:

LO QUE OCCURIÓ:

EFFECTOS:

Translated by P. Lerwick

Kingore, B. (2008). *Teaching Without Nonsense*, 2nd ed. Austin, TX: Professional Associates Publishing.

Event Map:
Tier II

On the back, record the resources you used. Then, use sentences and/or symbols to complete the map.

MAIN EVENT:

SETTING:

RELATED HISTORY:

HISTORICAL FIGURE:

PERSONAL:

PROFESSIONAL:

HISTORICAL FIGURE:

PERSONAL:

PROFESSIONAL:

Kingore, B. (2008). *Teaching Without Nonsense*, 2nd ed. Austin, TX: Professional Associates Publishing.

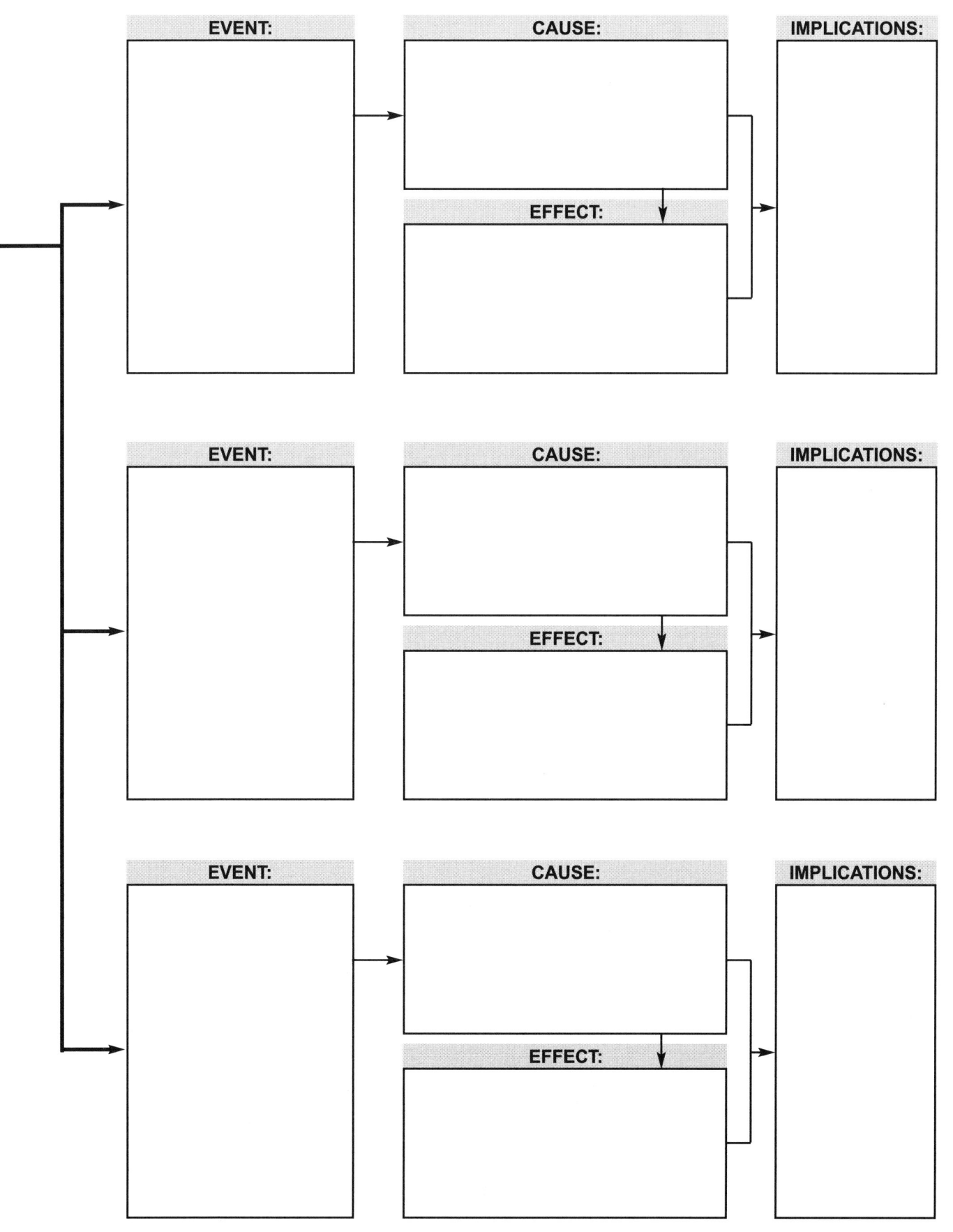

SECTION 2: Learning Experiences 63

EVENT:	CAUSE:	IMPLICATIONS:
	EFFECT:	

EVENT:	CAUSE:	IMPLICATIONS:
	EFFECT:	

EVENT:	CAUSE:	IMPLICATIONS:
	EFFECT:	

Kingore, B. (2008). *Teaching Without Nonsense*, 2nd ed. Austin, TX: Professional Associates Publishing.

Mapa del Evento:
Nivel II

En la parte de atrás, apunta los recursos o materiales que usaste. Después, utiliza oraciones o símbolos para terminar tu mapa.

EVENTO PRINCIPAL:

LUGAR:

RELACIÓN HISTÓRICA:

FIGURA HISTÓRICA:

PERSONAL:

PROFESIONAL:

FIGURA HISTÓRICA:

PERSONAL:

PROFESIONAL:

Kingore, B. (2008). *Teaching Without Nonsense*, 2nd ed. Austin, TX: Professional Associates Publishing.

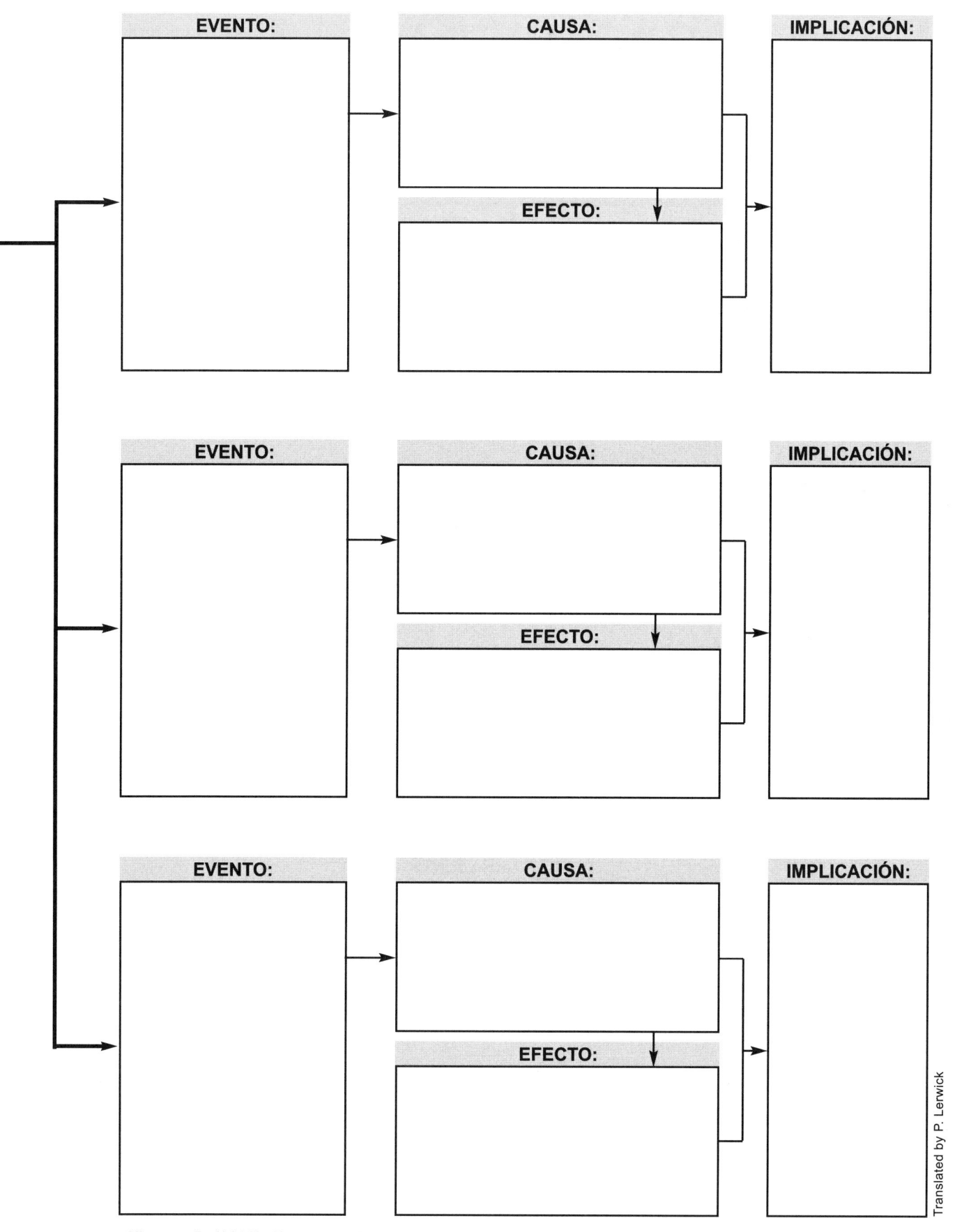

SECTION 2: Learning Experiences

EVENTO:	CAUSA:	IMPLICACIÓN:
	EFECTO:	

EVENTO:	CAUSA:	IMPLICACIÓN:
	EFECTO:	

EVENTO:	CAUSA:	IMPLICACIÓN:
	EFECTO:	

Translated by P. Lerwick

Kingore, B. (2008). *Teaching Without Nonsense*, 2nd ed. Austin, TX: Professional Associates Publishing.

Place Map

On the back, record the resources you used. Then, use sentences and/or symbols to complete the map.

PLACE:

DESCRIPTION:

INTERESTING FACTS:

IN THE PAST:

IN THE PRESENT:

IN THE FUTURE:

Kingore, B. (2008). *Teaching Without Nonsense*, 2nd ed. Austin, TX: Professional Associates Publishing.

SECTION 2: Learning Experiences

Esquema del Sitio

En la parte de atrás, apunta los recursos o materiales que usaste. Después, utiliza oraciones o símbolos para terminar tu mapa.

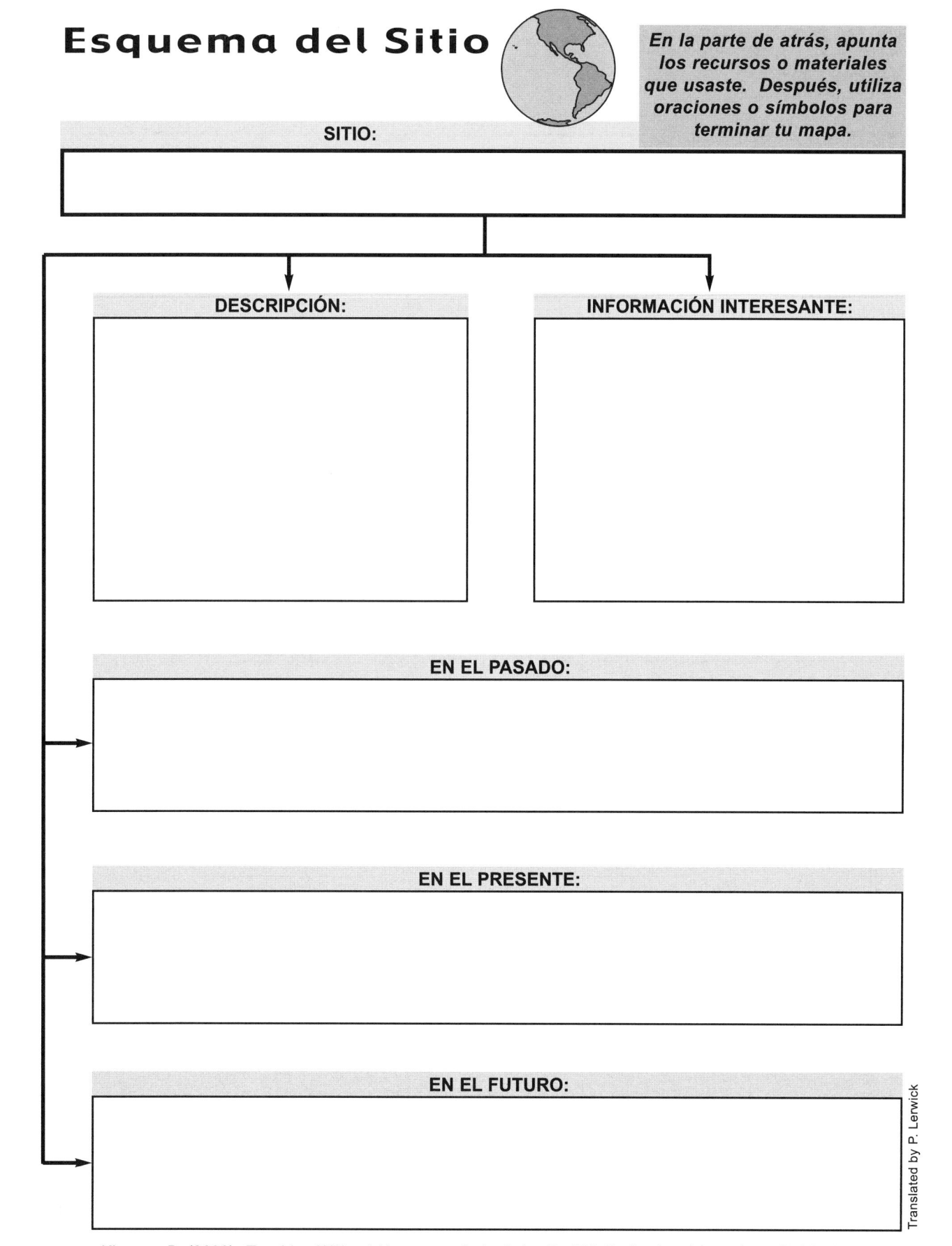

SITIO:

DESCRIPCIÓN:

INFORMACIÓN INTERESANTE:

EN EL PASADO:

EN EL PRESENTE:

EN EL FUTURO:

Translated by P. Lerwick

Kingore, B. (2008). *Teaching Without Nonsense*, 2nd ed. Austin, TX: Professional Associates Publishing.

Person Map:
Tier I

On the back, record the resources you used. Then, use sentences and/or symbols to complete the map.

PERSON:

CHILDHOOD AND FAMILY:

TRAITS:

IMPORTANCE:

ADULT LIFE:

Kingore, B. (2008). *Teaching Without Nonsense*, 2nd ed. Austin, TX: Professional Associates Publishing.

Croquis Personal:
Nivel I

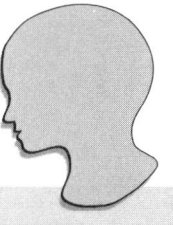

PERSONA:

En la parte de atrás, apunta los recursos o materiales que usaste. Después, utiliza oraciones o símbolos para terminar tu mapa.

NIÑEZ Y FAMILIA:

CARACTERÍSTICAS:

IMPORTANCIA:

EDAD ADULTA:

Translated by P. Lerwick

Kingore, B. (2008). *Teaching Without Nonsense*, 2nd ed. Austin, TX: Professional Associates Publishing.

Person Map:
Tier II

On the back, record the resources you used. Then, use sentences and/or symbols to complete the map.

PERSON:

YOUTH/PAST:
- SETTING:
- EVENTS:

MID-LIFE/PRESENT:
- SETTING:
- EVENTS:

OLDER/FUTURE:
- SETTING:
- EVENTS:

Kingore, B. (2008). *Teaching Without Nonsense*, 2nd ed. Austin, TX: Professional Associates Publishing.

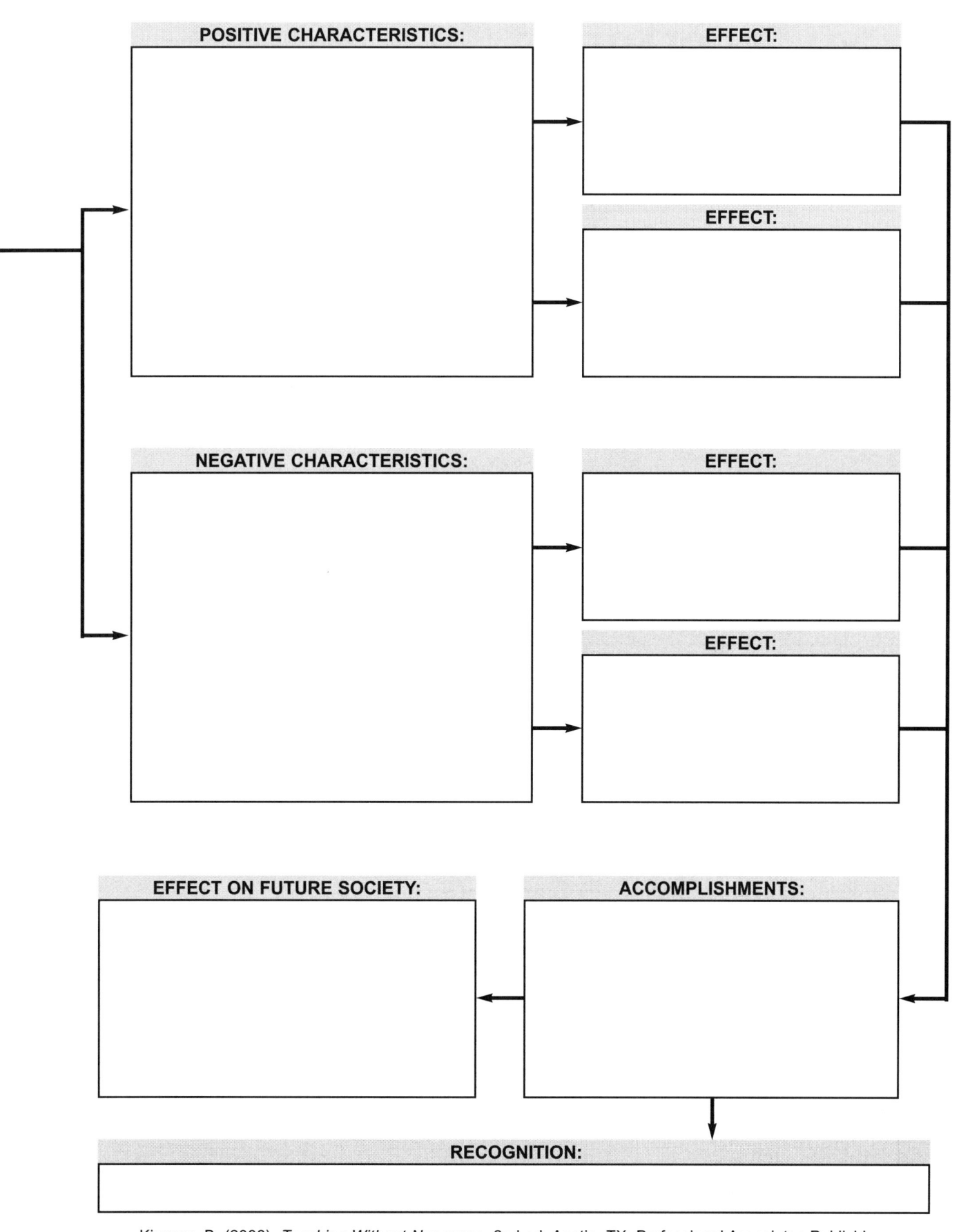

SECTION 2: Learning Experiences

POSITIVE CHARACTERISTICS:

EFFECT:

EFFECT:

NEGATIVE CHARACTERISTICS:

EFFECT:

EFFECT:

EFFECT ON FUTURE SOCIETY:

ACCOMPLISHMENTS:

RECOGNITION:

Kingore, B. (2008). *Teaching Without Nonsense*, 2nd ed. Austin, TX: Professional Associates Publishing.

Croquis Personal:
Nivel II

En la parte de atrás, apunta los recursos o materiales que usaste. Después, utiliza oraciones o símbolos para terminar tu mapa.

PERSONA:

JUVENTUD/ EL PASADO:
- LUGAR:
- EVENTOS:

EDAD MEDIA/ EL PRESENTE:
- LUGAR:
- EVENTOS:

VEJEZ/ EL FUTURO:
- LUGAR:
- EVENTOS:

Kingore, B. (2008). *Teaching Without Nonsense*, 2nd ed. Austin, TX: Professional Associates Publishing.

SECTION 2: Learning Experiences 73

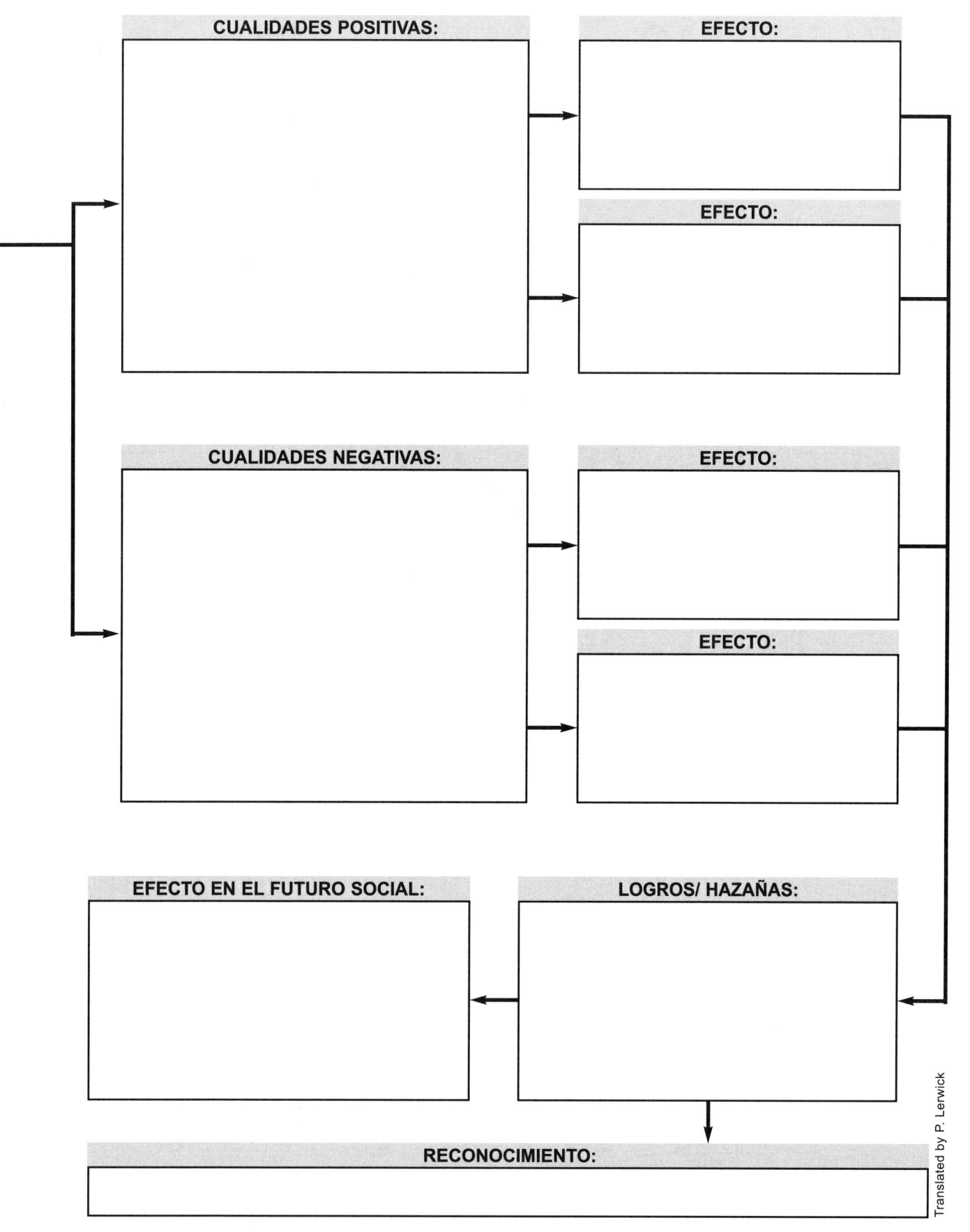

CUALIDADES POSITIVAS:	EFECTO:
	EFECTO:

CUALIDADES NEGATIVAS:	EFECTO:
	EFECTO:

EFECTO EN EL FUTURO SOCIAL:	LOGROS/ HAZAÑAS:

RECONOCIMIENTO:

Translated by P. Lerwick

Kingore, B. (2008). *Teaching Without Nonsense*, 2nd ed. Austin, TX: Professional Associates Publishing.

Rectangle Concept Map

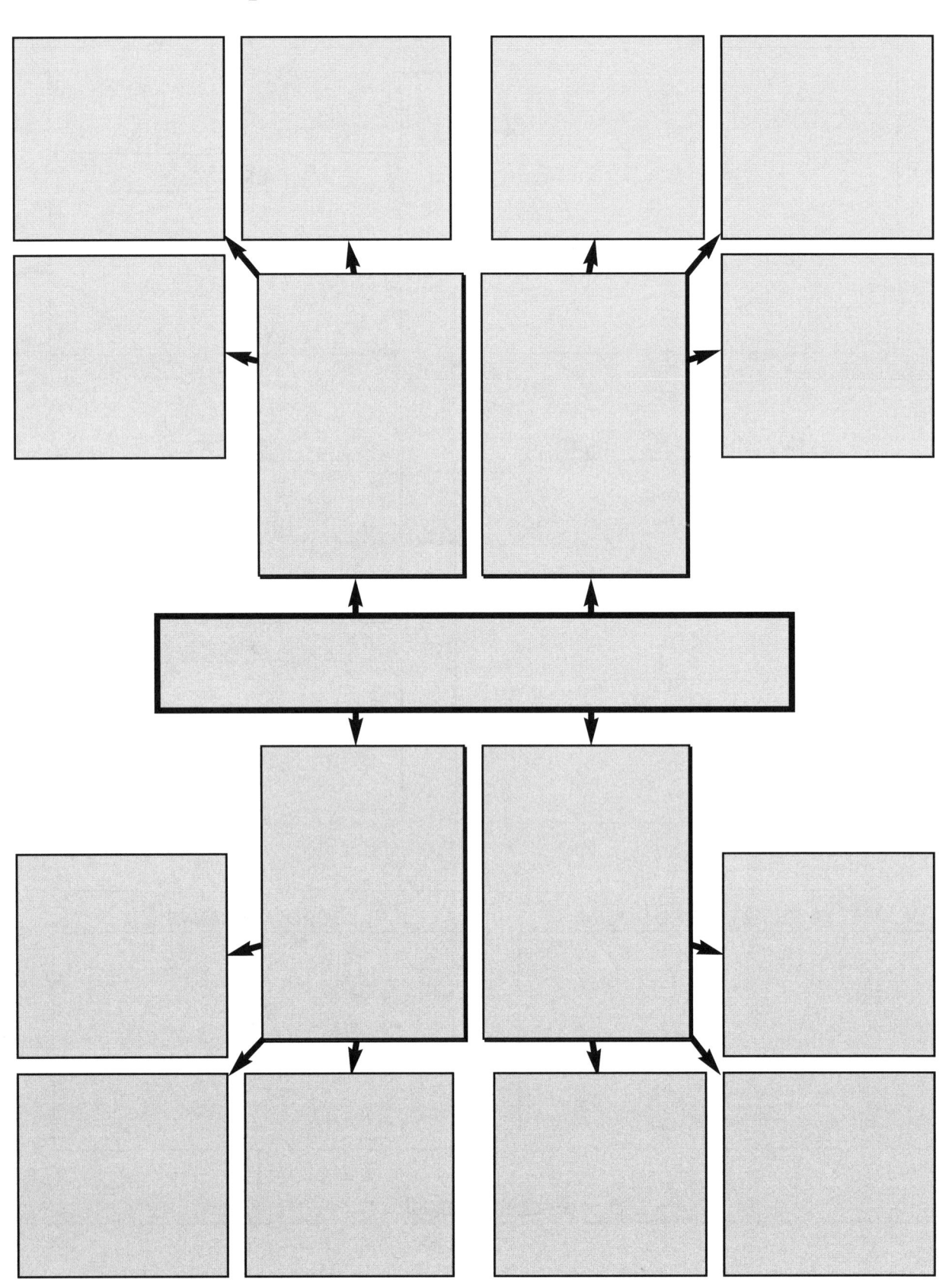

Kingore, B. (2008). *Teaching Without Nonsense*, 2nd ed. Austin, TX: Professional Associates Publishing.

SECTION 2: Learning Experiences

Fact Puzzle

Grade Levels: K-12

Kindergartners complete this task with adult facilitation

A fact puzzle learning experience:
- Provides a simple-to-prepare activity that connects to a myriad of topics, content areas, and skills.
- Serves as springboards for topic discussions, vocabulary development, summarization, and review.
- Promotes students' application, analysis, and synthesis.
- Encourages students to list resources as they acquire and organize information.
- Applies spelling skills.
- Serves as an assessment tool to assess accuracy, depth, and complexity of information.

Fact puzzles are a creative combination of acrostic and crossword puzzles. They are like acrostic because they use a concept or topic word to organize connected ideas. However, the letters of the concept word(s) appear anywhere in the line of the response rather than as the beginning letter. Similar to a crossword puzzle, fact puzzles incorporate informative phrases and questions to prompt the responses that need to be included.

Model how to complete a fact puzzle to teach students the process.
1. Select one of the provided examples of a fact puzzle or develop a simple puzzle using content the class is reviewing.
2. Show a copy of a fact puzzle on the computer, chalkboard, overhead, or chart. The

---

Fact Puzzle

RESOURCE(S): Stone Fox by John Reynolds Gardiner

1. Stone Fox is a _____ _____ recognized as the best dogsled racer in the country.
2. Willy, the _____ in the story, is a young boy who lives with his grandfather on a farm in Wyoming.
3. Willy is determined to keep his grandfather _____.
4. Willy needs $500 to pay _____. That is the exact amount of the prize from the National Dogsled Race!
5. _____ is the only hope Willy has to help him save the farm.
6. A short cut across a _____ puts Willy in the lead, but trouble is right behind him.
7. Willy _____ the last ten feet to finish the race.

N <u>a t i v e</u> <u>A m e r i c a n</u>

p r <u>O t a g o n i s t</u>

<u>a l i V e</u>

<u>t a x E s</u>

<u>S e a r c h L i g h t</u>

<u>L a k e</u>

<u>W A l k e d</u>

Kingore, B. (2008). *Teaching Without Nonsense*, 2nd ed. Austin, TX: Professional Associates Publishing.

Kingore, B. (2008). *Teaching Without Nonsense*, 2nd ed. Austin, TX: Professional Associates Publishing.

content must be well understood by the group so they can successfully participate.
3. Point out how each line provides a statement or question to cue the appropriate response. Each answer must fit in the spaces and match the letter provided for that line.
4. Read the first cue together and write the answer in the correct spaces when students figure it out.
5. Continue with the next line.
6. As students demonstrate understanding, have them work in pairs to figure out the next line and continue until the puzzle is complete.
7. As a closure, review the process together to prepare students to work other fact puzzles with less direct instruction. Ask them to brainstorm additional applications, such as other topics to use to develop new fact puzzles. Discuss adding illustrations to increase the visual appeal of the puzzle.

Examples of several fact puzzles are included on the following pages. The answers to those puzzles are listed here.

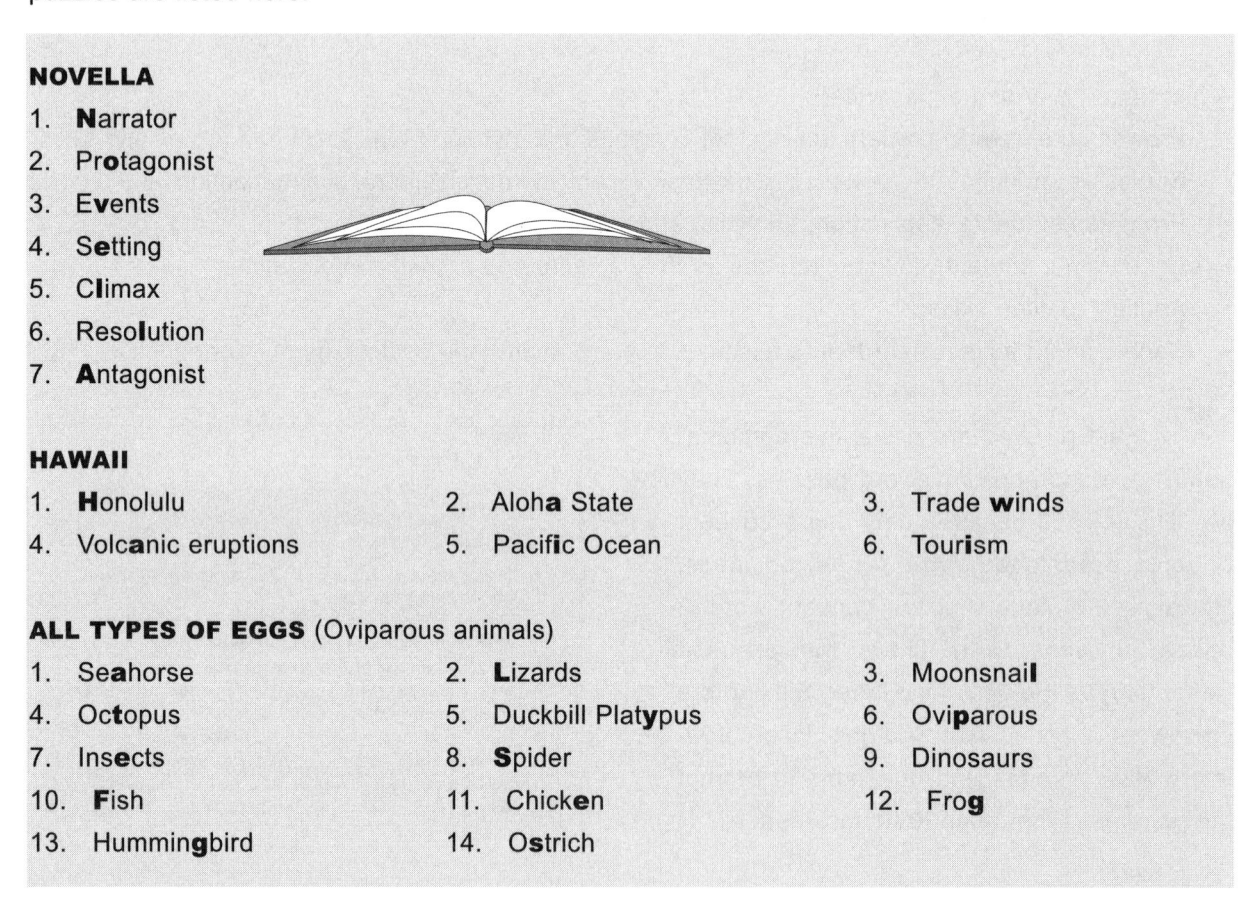

NOVELLA
1. **N**arrator
2. P**r**otagonist
3. **E**vents
4. S**e**tting
5. C**l**imax
6. Reso**l**ution
7. **A**ntagonist

HAWAII
1. **H**onolulu
2. Aloh**a** State
3. Trade **w**inds
4. Vol**c**anic eruptions
5. Pac**i**fic Ocean
6. Tour**i**sm

ALL TYPES OF EGGS (Oviparous animals)
1. Se**a**horse
2. **L**izards
3. Moonsnai**l**
4. Octopus
5. Duckbill Pla**t**ypus
6. Ovi**p**arous
7. Ins**e**cts
8. **S**pider
9. Dinosaurs
10. **F**ish
11. Chick**e**n
12. Fro**g**
13. Hummin**g**bird
14. O**s**trich

Variations

- Promote depth and complexity by requiring students to record their sources of information when completing a fact puzzle. Teachers find that students' responses are more specific and elaborative when encouraged to incorporate multiple resources.

Kingore, B. (2008). *Teaching Without Nonsense*, 2nd ed. Austin, TX: Professional Associates Publishing.

- The Novella example is adaptable to most works of fiction. Using content from a different book, write applicable statements or questions about the story or a character to cue answers that include the same letters as those provided in the example. This variation is effective as a closure task after completing a novel.

- To review content and demonstrate understanding, challenge students to work in pairs or trios to develop original fact puzzles for other students to complete. To create a fact puzzle, students must understand the content, determine the most significant information, and plan how to organize it into a puzzle. Teachers report that the quality and complexity of the puzzles' content increase when students prepare puzzles that other students must complete.

- Instead of using the provided novella example with literary terminology, promote students' understanding by having them create the puzzle. Invite small groups of students to write definitions or examples of each literary term to list as the statements cuing the words in the fact puzzle.

- Require students to apply inference skills by covering the title of a fact puzzle before presenting it to a small group. As students consider the facts, they decipher the topic.

- When students are creating original fact puzzles, increase their level and depth of thinking by challenging them to determine the main idea or theme, and then use that as the acrostic for organizing the content responses.

- Challenge students to prepare fact puzzles as products that synthesize and organize their research of a topic.

- Skillfully construct a fact puzzle as a pre- and post-evaluation. Rather than a narrow list of facts, the content should emphasize the key points that express the intended learning objectives.

Options for Implementation

Error Analysis

Provide a fact puzzle with three or more information or skill errors. As a closure task, inform the class that there is misinformation or mistakes in the puzzle without telling them the total number of errors. Students work in pairs or trios for two minutes to determine which errors they can identify and explain how to correct. Many students respond enthusiastically to finding others' errors.

This error analysis option is particularly applicable for spelling skills. The novelty of providing key vocabulary that is spelled incorrectly stimulates students' attention to spelling.

Kingore, B. (2008). *Teaching Without Nonsense*, 2nd ed. Austin, TX: Professional Associates Publishing.

Fact Puzzle Tiering Chart

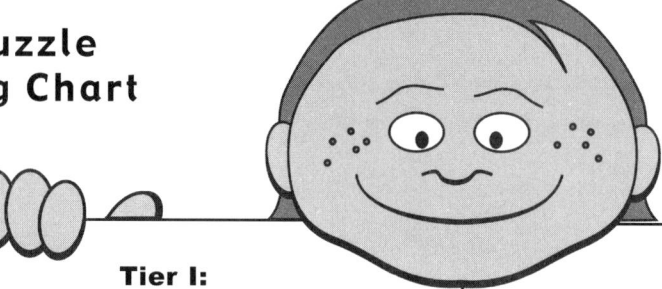

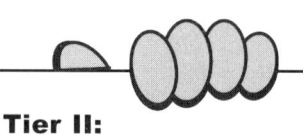

Tier I: Simpler Applications

The teacher scribes the children's ideas on the CD template or a paper copy.

An adult facilitates or pairs of students work together to successfully complete a fact puzzle.

Individuals complete a fact puzzle that has simple, basic content.

Individuals or pairs of students create a fact puzzle using grade-level resources and information.

The response uses words and phrases that are spelled correctly and are accurate but basic.

Tier II: More Complex Applications

Individuals complete a fact puzzle that has more abstract or complex content.

To complete or create a fact puzzle, the students use provided resources that are complex with beyond grade-level information.

Individuals or pairs of students develop a fact puzzle using beyond grade-level resources and information that they access and research.

The fact puzzle uses correctly-spelled words and phrases that are more complex and use multi-syllable, topic-specific vocabulary.

Kingore, B. (2008). *Teaching Without Nonsense*, 2nd ed. Austin, TX: Professional Associates Publishing.

Fact Puzzle

RESOURCE(S):

NOVELLA

1. Who tells the story when it is written in third-person point of view?
2. What is the term for the character who is hero?
3. The _____ develop the story line and sequence the story.
4. The _____ is the time and place of the story.
5. The main conflicts of the story come together at the _____.
6. The _____ is the term conveying when the problem or dispute is solved.
7. What is the term for the opposition or adversary in the story?

N _ _ _ _ _ _ _

_ _ O _ _ _ _ _ _ _ _

_ V _ _ _ _

_ E _ _ _ _ _

_ L _ _ _ _

_ _ _ _ L _ _ _ _ _

A _ _ _ _ _ _ _ _ _

Kingore, B. (2008). *Teaching Without Nonsense*, 2nd ed. Austin, TX: Professional Associates Publishing.

Fact Puzzle

RESOURCE(S):

HAWAII

1. What is the capital?
2. Hawaii is also known as the _____ _____.
3. The mild climate is due to _____ _____.
4. _____ _____ created the islands.
5. Hawaii is located in the _____ _____.
6. What is the leading industry in Hawaii?

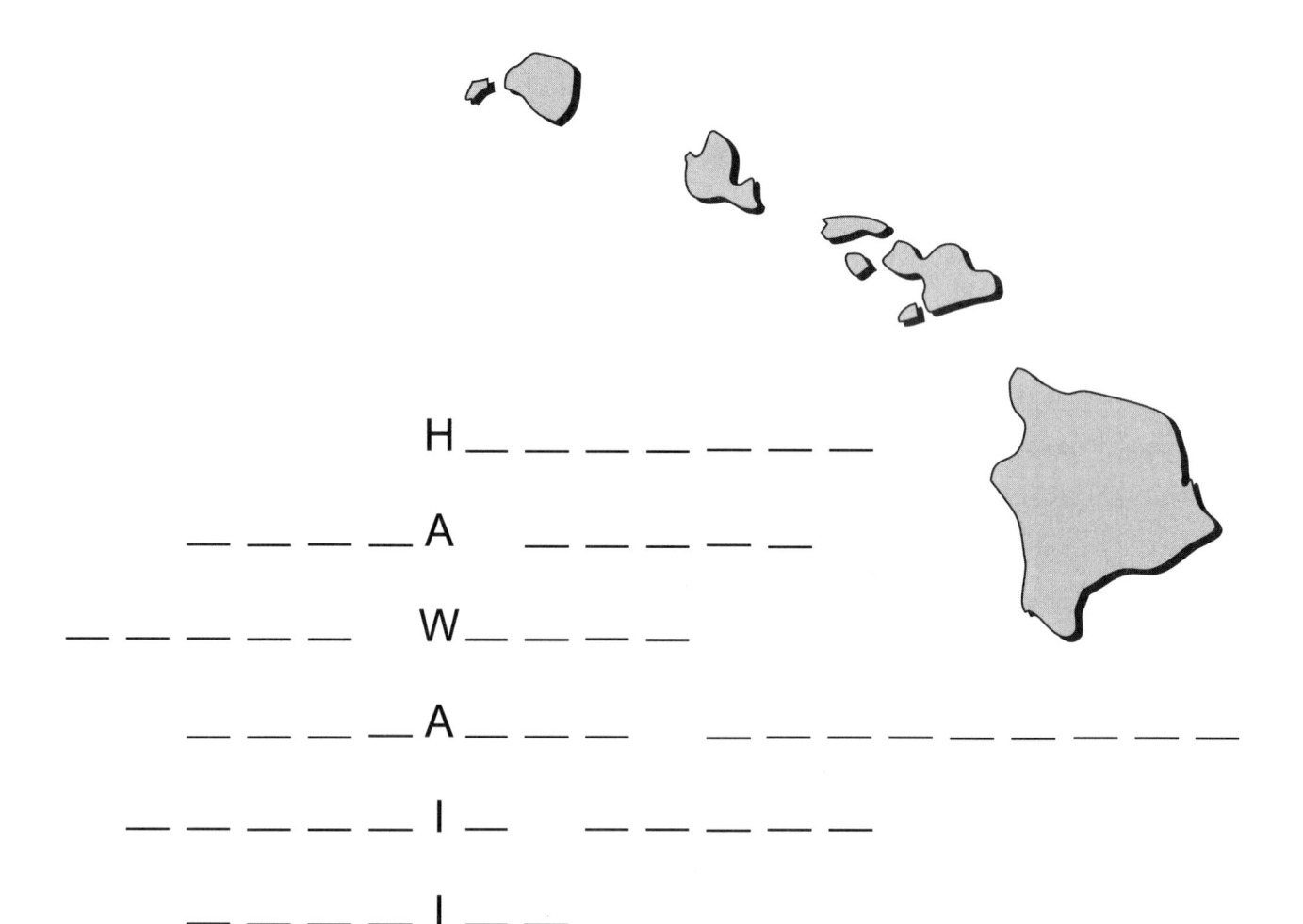

```
H _ _ _ _ _ _

_ _ _ _ A _ _ _ _ _ _

_ _ _ _ _ W _ _ _ _

_ _ _ _ A _ _ _   _ _ _ _ _ _ _ _ _

_ _ _ _ _ I _   _ _ _ _ _

_ _ _ _ I _ _
```

Kingore, B. (2008). *Teaching Without Nonsense*, 2nd ed. Austin, TX: Professional Associates Publishing.

Fact Puzzle

RESOURCE(S):

1. The father carries the eggs in a special pouch until they hatch.
2. These modern-day reptiles lay eggs.
3. It mixes its eggs with sand to form a collar-looking band.
4. It sheds one hundred thousand eggs and hangs them from rocks and caves.
5. This mammal lays eggs and lives in Australia.
6. This is the scientific term for every animal that lays eggs.
7. They have six legs and lay all types of eggs.
8. It wraps its eggs in sacs.
9. These extinct reptiles laid eggs long ago.
10. Their eggs float to the surface or sink to the bottom of the sea.
11. We often eat this bird's eggs.
12. This amphibian lays eggs.
13. This bird lays the smallest egg of all the birds.
14. This bird lays the largest egg.

OVIPAROUS ANIMALS

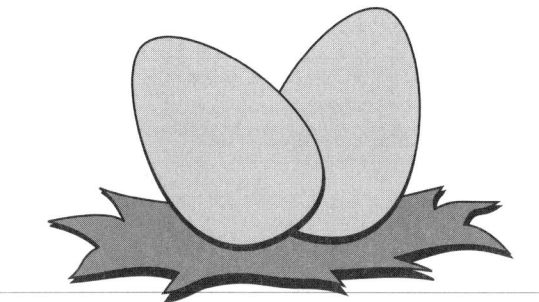

1. __ __ A __ __ __ __ __
2. L __ __ __ __ __ __
3. __ __ __ __ __ __ __ __ L
4. __ __ T __ __ __ __
5. __ __ __ __ __ __ __ __ __   __ __ __ Y __ __ __
6. __ __ __ P __ __ __ __
7. __ __ __ E __ __ __
8. S __ __ __ __ __ __
9. __ __ __ O __ __ __ __
10. F __ __ __
11. __ __ __ __ __ E __
12. __ __ __ G
13. __ __ __ __ __ G __ __ __
14. __ S __ __ __ __ __

Kingore, B. (2008). *Teaching Without Nonsense*, 2nd ed. Austin, TX: Professional Associates Publishing.

I Am

Grade Levels: K-12

Beginning writing skills are required in order for kindergartners to complete this task.

The I Am learning experience:
- Connects topics of study to students' lives and experiences.
- Serves as a springboard for topic discussions, vocabulary development, summarization, and content review.
- Promotes multiple points of view through first-person writing and personification.
- Applies inference skills.
- Promotes conceptual thinking more than recall or simple thinking.
- Serves as an assessment tool to assess students' accuracy, depth, and complexity of content.

I Am is a scaffold for organizing students' feelings and connecting information. The simple sentence stems prompt analytical responses about self and other topics. Included on the pages that follow are three tiers of I Am forms that enable teachers to differentiate the complexity of the learning experience to match students' capabilities. The simplest is brief; the next level allows more expanded analysis and encourages the use of adjectives; the third invites more complex syntax, synonyms, and metaphorical thinking. Vary the sentence stems on these examples to develop customized versions that guide students' analysis of specific content.

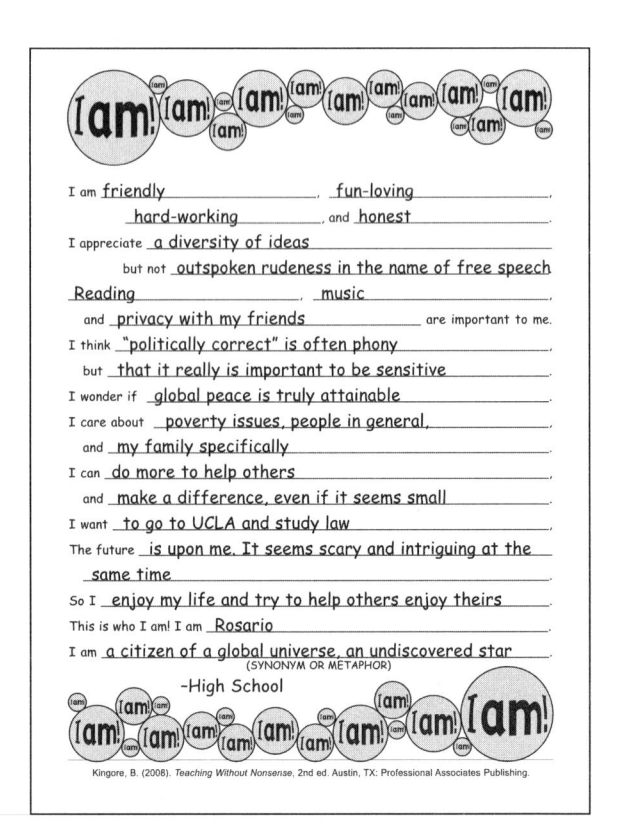

I am _friendly_, _fun-loving_, _hard-working_, and _honest_.
I appreciate _a diversity of ideas_
but not _outspoken rudeness in the name of free speech_.
Reading, _music_, and _privacy with my friends_ are important to me.
I think _"politically correct" is often phony_,
but _that it really is important to be sensitive_.
I wonder if _global peace is truly attainable_.
I care about _poverty issues, people in general_,
and _my family specifically_.
I can _do more to help others_
and _make a difference, even if it seems small_.
I want _to go to UCLA and study law_.
The future _is upon me. It seems scary and intriguing at the same time_.
So I _enjoy my life and try to help others enjoy theirs_.
This is who I am! I am _Rosario_.
I am _a citizen of a global universe, an undiscovered star_.
(SYNONYM OR METAPHOR)
–High School

Kingore, B. (2008). *Teaching Without Nonsense*, 2nd ed. Austin, TX: Professional Associates Publishing.

Kingore, B. (2008). *Teaching Without Nonsense*, 2nd ed. Austin, TX: Professional Associates Publishing.

To model the I Am learning experience, think aloud and list ideas about yourself as the class listens. Demonstrate how to organize and record those ideas on one of the tiers. Then, ask students to brainstorm and list ideas about themselves on a planning sheet before they complete the most applicable I Am tier. Challenge students to use more advanced and content specific vocabulary when appropriate. The results are interesting to share among class members or to post for other students and adults to read. (Advise students before they begin the learning experience if their I Am products will be posted or shared in any way.)

For closure, challenge students to analyze their process as they complete an I Am. Which line caused them to pause and ponder? Did they complete each line in sequence or did they skip around as they thought of ideas? Elicit any ideas they have for changing the prompts on any line.

As students understand the process and gain confidence in their applications, progress from more concrete personal applications and writing about a researched historical or current figure, to more abstract analysis of a character in a story, and ultimately, to a personification of a topic, such as: *I am multiplication*. Initially, allow students to work in pairs or trios for support or to encourage multiple perspectives and a richer pool of information. Typically, discussion and negotiation become critical in completing this small group process and further enhance students' integration of information about a topic.

Personification or topical applications of I Am have the potential to incorporate the greatest complexity and abstract thinking. They require a unique perspective to a topic as students elaborate ideas and organize information. Eventually, many students use and complete these tiers without direct teacher instruction. At that point, I Am provides an effective product for students' research projects and individual study.

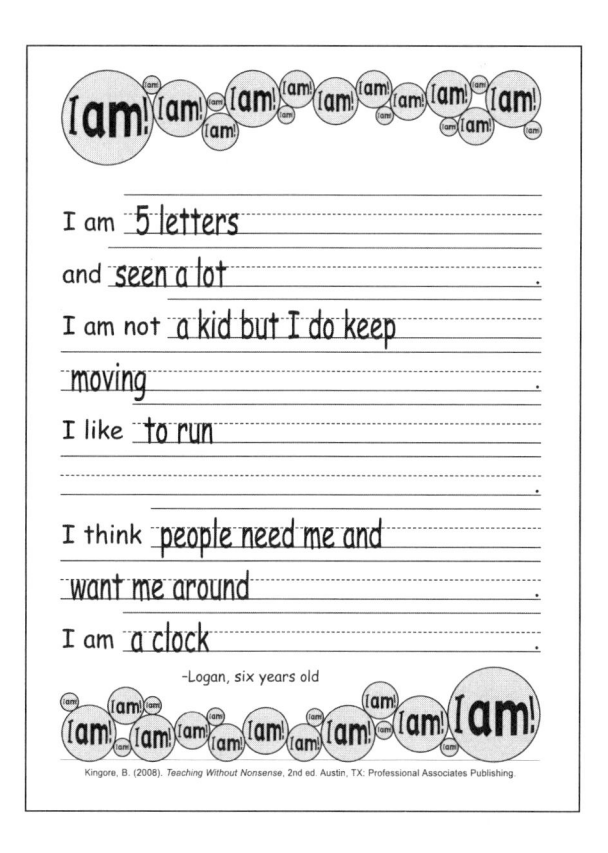

> I am 5 letters
> and seen a lot.
> I am not a kid but I do keep moving.
> I like to run.
> I think people need me and want me around.
> I am a clock.
> —Logan, six years old

Kingore, B. (2008). *Teaching Without Nonsense*, 2nd ed. Austin, TX: Professional Associates Publishing.

Variations

- I Am products about self become insightful, comparative pieces when students complete an I Am at the beginning and then again at the end of the school year. These repeated products are effective portfolio items to emphasize affective as well as academic changes in each student.

Kingore, B. (2008). *Teaching Without Nonsense*, 2nd ed. Austin, TX: Professional Associates Publishing.

- Combine the I Am writing task with art applications. After writing an I Am about themselves, students use the written page as the trunk of their cut-paper figure. With construction paper, they create heads, arms, legs, and add extensive identifying details such as hair color, glasses, and favorite style of clothing and shoes. These cut-paper figures make an intriguing display that challenges observers to identify each student. They are an audience-pleasing choice to display for parents during a school open house or curriculum night.

- With ELL and dual language learners, challenge students to complete an I Am in more than one language. Compare and discuss the process to emphasize the similarities and differences in the syntax and vocabulary of the languages.

- Guide students to review a completed example of the most complex template for I Am. Identify cause and effect relationships within the content.

- Use the I Am form to have students retell a process, such as conducting a science experiment or applying a math strategy. The I Am for rounding numbers is one example.

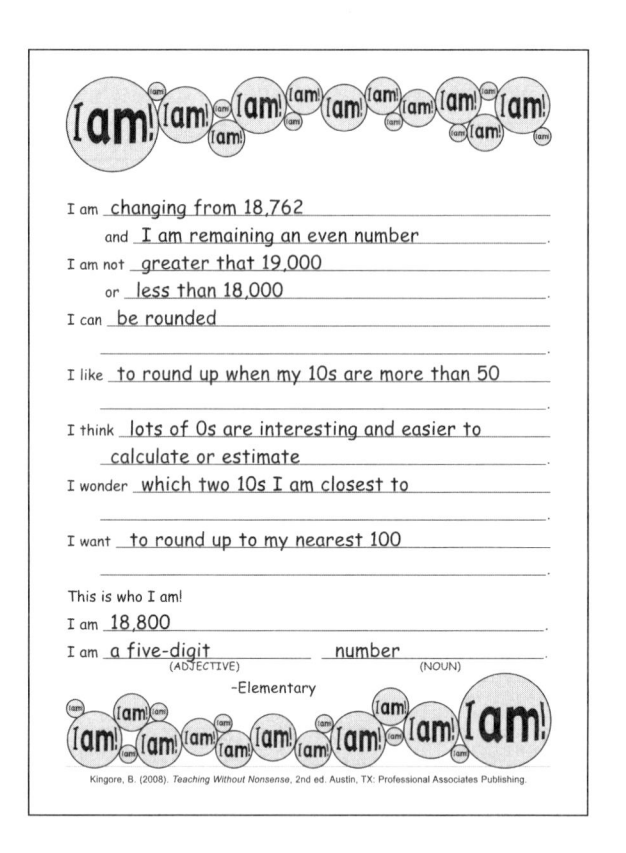

Sample I Am form:

I am changing from 18,762
  and I am remaining an even number.
I am not greater that 19,000
  or less than 18,000.
I can be rounded
I like to round up when my 10s are more than 50
I think lots of 0s are interesting and easier to calculate or estimate
I wonder which two 10s I am closest to
I want to round up to my nearest 100
This is who I am!
I am 18,800
I am a five-digit (ADJECTIVE) number (NOUN)
-Elementary

Kingore, B. (2008). *Teaching Without Nonsense*, 2nd ed. Austin, TX: Professional Associates Publishing.

Options for Implementation

Content Review

Use a topical I Am as an interactive review technique applicable to multiple aspects of a topic. Ask students to stand. Then, read one line at a time of an information-rich I Am about a current topic of study as a riddle game for students to figure out before the last line is revealed. For example, the lines reveal different characters from books the class has read or different species from a study of rain forest flora and fauna.

As each line is read, students sit down when they have figured out the topic. Ask seated students to write and then show their answer on an individual response board, such as a chalkboard or wipe-off board. If the correct topic is identified, the game is finished. If the answer is incorrect, the boards are wiped off, students stand again, and the game continues.

Kingore, B. (2008). *Teaching Without Nonsense*, 2nd ed. Austin, TX: Professional Associates Publishing.

Inference Skills

As a guided practice of inference skills, read aloud completed I Am examples that students write about themselves. Randomly select an I Am from the class set and read one sentence from that student's I Am without identifying the student. Simultaneously, students number a paper from one to three, and beside numeral one, they write the name of the student they think fits the shared information. Then, read another sentence from the I Am and ask students to write beside numeral two the name of the student they think fits both clues. Briefly discuss who elected to change an answer as additional information is shared. Elicit students' reasons for changing responses. Discuss how additional information affects inferential thinking. Continue the process with another clue before revealing the student's name.

Sharing only three clues for any one student enables a faster-paced process and involves more students' products. It also allows the reader to select the clues that will have the greatest potential for inferential thinking.

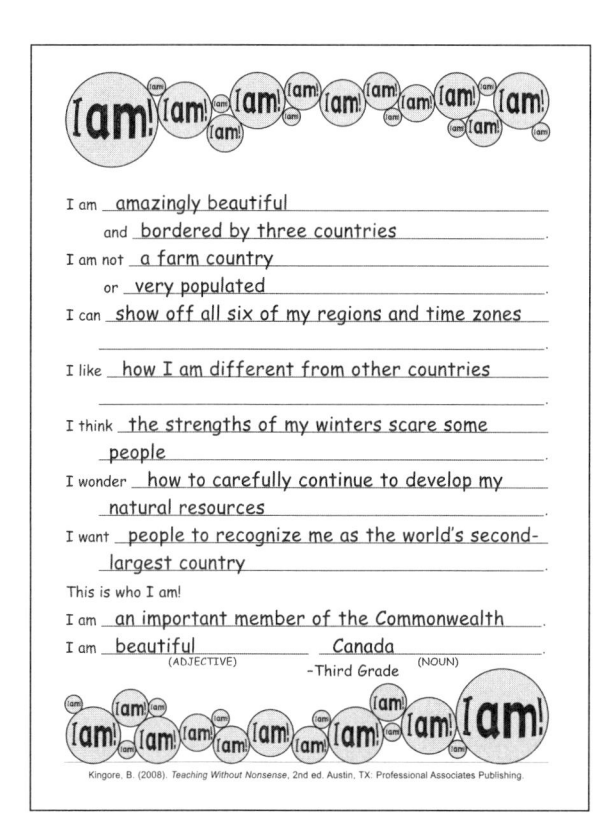

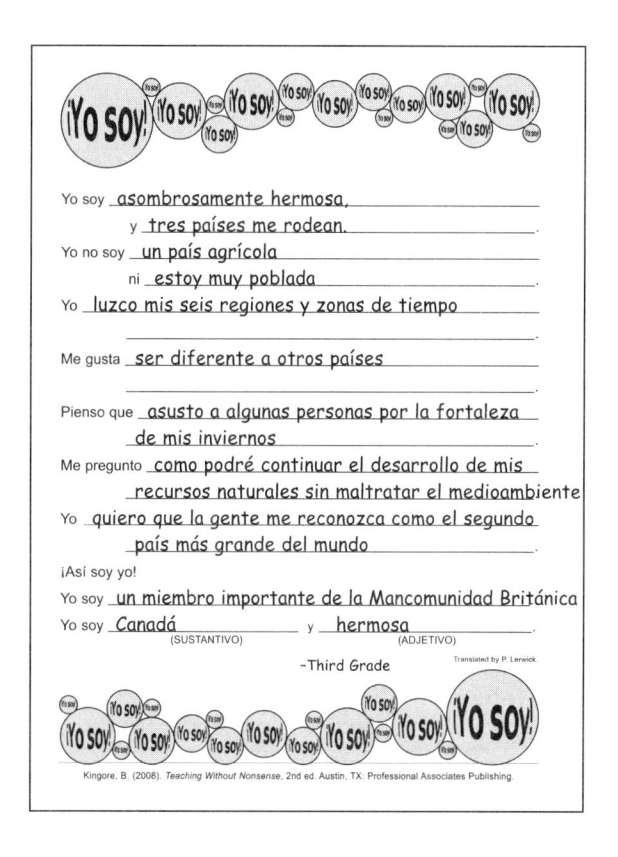

I am amazingly beautiful
  and bordered by three countries.
I am not a farm country
  or very populated.
I can show off all six of my regions and time zones

I like how I am different from other countries

I think the strengths of my winters scare some
  people.
I wonder how to carefully continue to develop my
  natural resources.
I want people to recognize me as the world's second-
  largest country.
This is who I am!
I am an important member of the Commonwealth
I am beautiful   Canada
        (ADJECTIVE)   (NOUN)
              -Third Grade

Yo soy asombrosamente hermosa,
  y tres países me rodean.
Yo no soy un país agrícola
  ni estoy muy poblada.
Yo luzco mis seis regiones y zonas de tiempo

Me gusta ser diferente a otros países

Pienso que asusto a algunas personas por la fortaleza
  de mis inviernos.
Me pregunto como podré continuar el desarrollo de mis
  recursos naturales sin maltratar el medioambiente.
Yo quiero que la gente me reconozca como el segundo
  país más grande del mundo.
¡Así soy yo!
Yo soy un miembro importante de la Mancomunidad Británica
Yo soy Canadá   y hermosa
        (SUSTANTIVO)   (ADJETIVO)
              -Third Grade   Translated by P. Lerwick

Kingore, B. (2008). *Teaching Without Nonsense*, 2nd ed. Austin, TX: Professional Associates Publishing.

I am!

I am _shiny_
  and _made of metal_.
I am not _silver_
  or _gold_.
I can _be added to others_

I like _Abraham Lincoln_

I think _I am important but some people don't value me_

I wonder _how many of me it takes to buy things_

I want _other coins to want me_

This is who I am!
I am _a penny_.
I am _a one-cent_ _coin_
       (ADJECTIVE)   (NOUN)

—First Grade

I am!

I am _fast_, _strong_,
  brave, and _black_.
I appreciate _the freedom to participate in activities_
  but not _sitting on the side lines and watching others play_
Running, _competing_,
  and _winning_ are important to me.
I think _it is important to persevere through hard times_,
  but _that doesn't mean it will be easy_
I wonder if _I had never walked, what would my life be?_
I care about _training other athletes to succeed_
  and _helping them overcome their circumstances_
I can _help them have confidence_
  and _help their dreams come true_
I want _to make a difference in the lives of others_
The future _holds many adventures for us all if we are not afraid to take risks_
So I _am going to leap toward my dream_
This is who I am! I am _Wilma Rudolph_
I am _a gazelle and Olympic gold medalist_
       (SYNONYM OR METAPHOR)

—Middle School

I am!

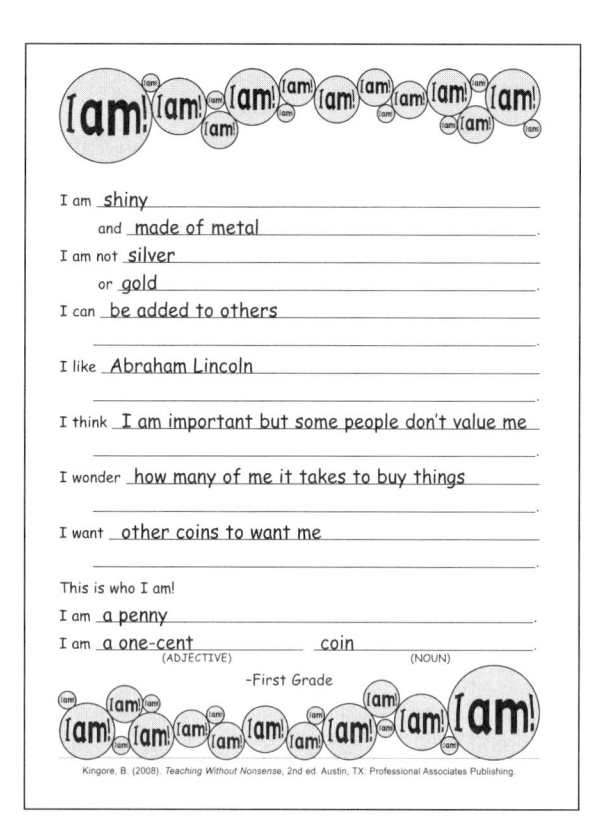

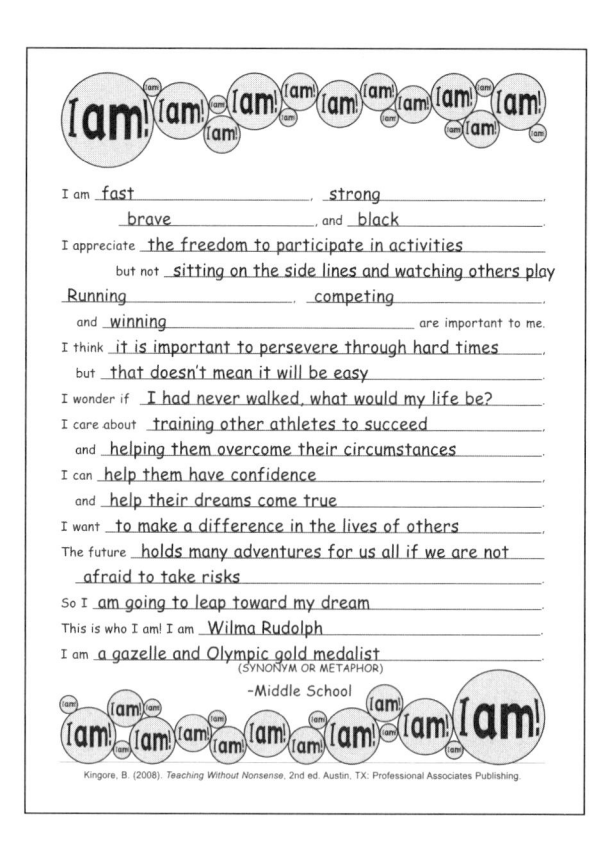

I am _wages_, _labor_,
  capital, and _fixed prices_.
I appreciate _returns to scale_
  but not _proportional changes in prices_
Marginal costs, _output_,
  and _marginal revenue_ are important to me.
I think _average cost will increase_,
  but _fear that average productivity will decrease_
I wonder if _supply will reach demand_
I care about _the producers' surplus_
  and _the society burden_
I can _expand the production possibilities curve with technology_
  and _become more efficient_
I want _to avoid diminishing marginal returns_
The future _is growth and expansion to new markets_

So I _advances in technology and productivity are vital_
This is who I am! I am _economics_
I am _the manufacturing of goods_
       (SYNONYM OR METAPHOR)

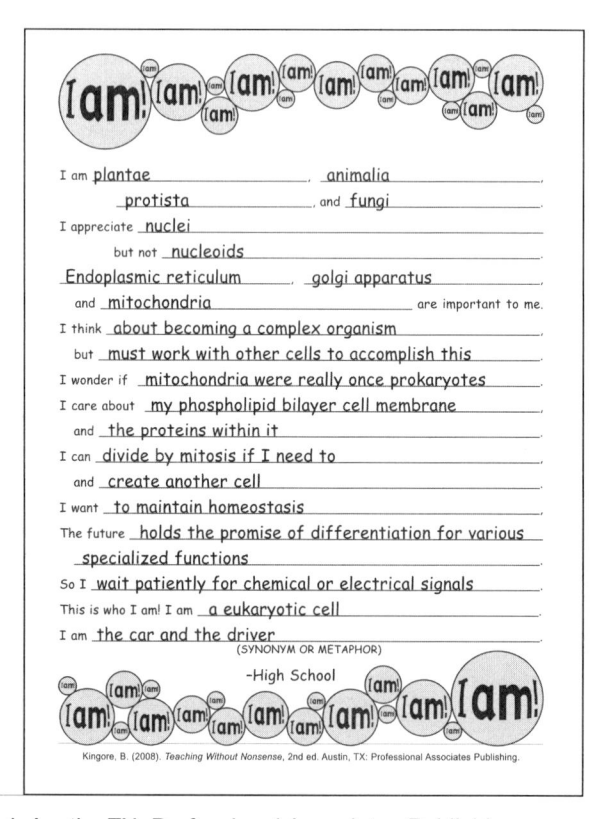

—High School

I am!

I am _plantae_, _animalia_,
  protista, and _fungi_.
I appreciate _nuclei_
  but not _nucleoids_
Endoplasmic reticulum, _golgi apparatus_,
  and _mitochondria_ are important to me.
I think _about becoming a complex organism_,
  but _must work with other cells to accomplish this_
I wonder if _mitochondria were really once prokaryotes_
I care about _my phospholipid bilayer cell membrane_
  and _the proteins within it_
I can _divide by mitosis if I need to_
  and _create another cell_
I want _to maintain homeostasis_
The future _holds the promise of differentiation for various specialized functions_
So I _wait patiently for chemical or electrical signals_
This is who I am! I am _a eukaryotic cell_
I am _the car and the driver_
       (SYNONYM OR METAPHOR)

—High School

Kingore, B. (2008). *Teaching Without Nonsense*, 2nd ed. Austin, TX: Professional Associates Publishing.

I Am Tiering Chart

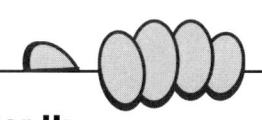

Tier I: Simpler Applications	Tier II: More Complex Applications
With adult support, students are guided to complete an I Am using the CD template or working on a paper copy.	Students complete a middle-level CD template or paper copy that personifies a topic.
Students use the simplest or middle-level template and add words or phrases to complete the task. As needed, support the process through teacher facilitation or pairs of students working together.	Students complete the most complex template, incorporating complex sentences that demonstrate high-level content.
The vocabulary is accurate but basic.	The vocabulary is more complex and applies multi-syllable words that are topic specific.
I Am is written about self.	Individuals or pairs of students complete a topic I Am about an abstract concept.
I Am is written about a fiction or nonfiction person other than self.	Individuals develop an I Am using the most complex template to document learning after accessing and researching information from beyond grade-level resources.

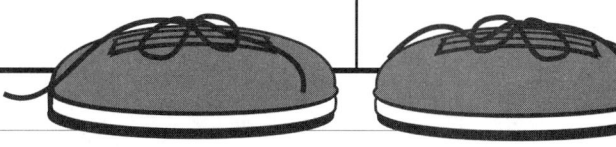

Kingore, B. (2008). *Teaching Without Nonsense*, 2nd ed. Austin, TX: Professional Associates Publishing.

I am _____

and _____.

I am not _____

_____.

I like _____

_____.

I think _____

_____.

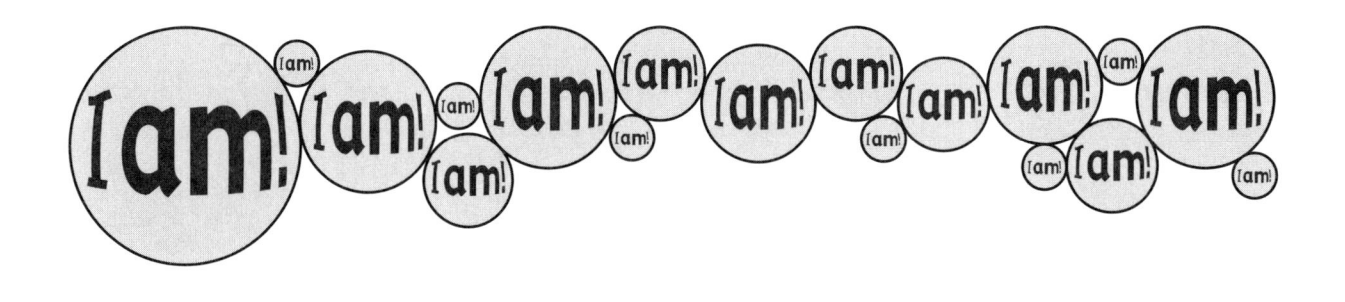

I am _____.

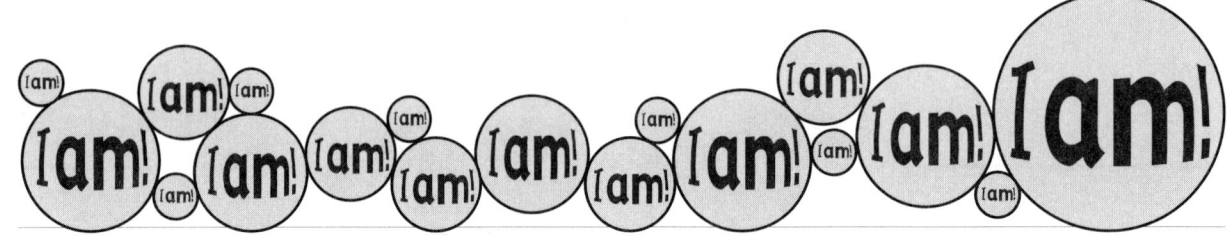

Kingore, B. (2008). *Teaching Without Nonsense*, 2nd ed. Austin, TX: Professional Associates Publishing.

SECTION 2: Learning Experiences

Yo soy _____

Y _____.

Yo no soy _____

_____.

Me gusta _____

_____.

Pienso que _____

_____.

Yo soy _____.

Translated by T. Spies and M. Bailey.

Kingore, B. (2008). *Teaching Without Nonsense*, 2nd ed. Austin, TX: Professional Associates Publishing.

I am _____
    and _____.
I am not _____
    or _____.
I can _____
_____.
I like _____
_____.
I think _____
_____.
I wonder _____
_____.
I want _____
_____.
This is who I am!
I am _____.
I am _____ _____.
         (ADJECTIVE)   (NOUN)

Kingore, B. (2008). *Teaching Without Nonsense*, 2nd ed. Austin, TX: Professional Associates Publishing.

Yo soy _____

        y _____.

Yo no soy _____

        ni _____.

Yo _____

_____.

Me gusta _____

_____.

Pienso que _____

_____.

Me pregunto _____

_____.

Yo _____

_____.

¡Así soy yo!

Yo soy _____.

Yo soy _____ y _____.
       (SUSTANTIVO)   (ADJETIVO)

Translated by T. Spies, M. Bailey, and P. Lerwick.

Kingore, B. (2008). *Teaching Without Nonsense*, 2nd ed. Austin, TX: Professional Associates Publishing.

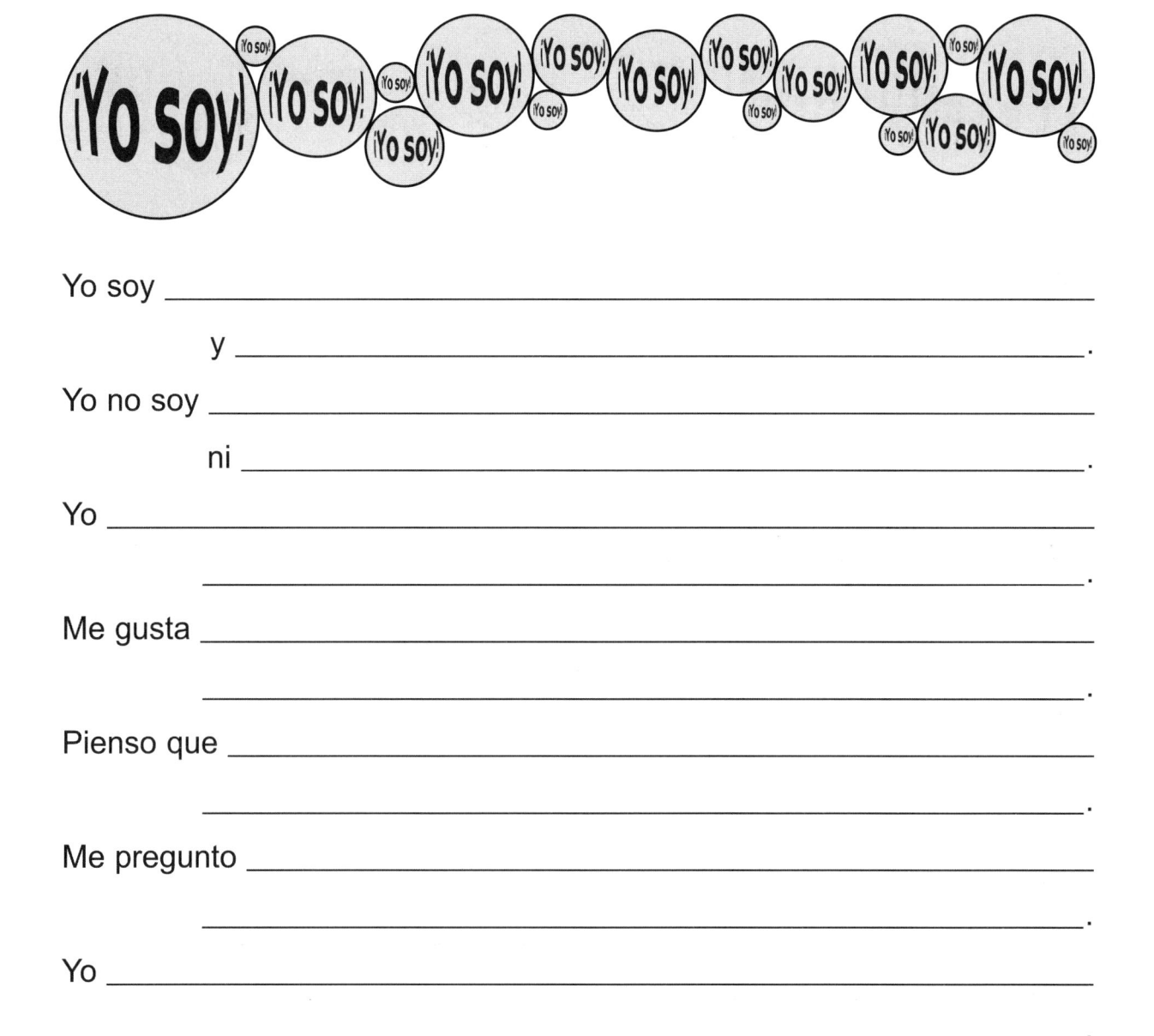

I am _____, _____,
_____, and _____.

I appreciate _____
    but not _____.

_____, _____,
    and _____ are important to me.

I think _____,
    but _____.

I wonder if _____.

I care about _____,
    and _____.

I can _____,
    and _____.

I want _____.

The future _____
_____.

So I _____.

This is who I am! I am _____.

I am _____.
           (SYNONYM OR METAPHOR)

Kingore, B. (2008). *Teaching Without Nonsense*, 2nd ed. Austin, TX: Professional Associates Publishing.

Yo soy _____, _____,
_____ y _____.

Aprecio _____

    pero no _____.

_____, _____

    y _____ es importante para mí.

Pienso que _____,

    pero _____.

Me pregunto si _____.

Me importa _____

    y _____.

Puedo _____

    y _____.

Deseo _____.

El futuro _____
_____.

Por eso, yo _____.

¡Así soy yo!

Yo soy _____.
(SINÓNIMO O METÁFORA)

Translated by T. Spies, M. Bailey, and P. Lerwick.

Kingore, B. (2008). *Teaching Without Nonsense*, 2nd ed. Austin, TX: Professional Associates Publishing.

Important Thing

Grade Levels: K-12

Kindergartners complete this task with adult facilitation.

The Important Thing learning experience:
- Encourages students to analyze, synthesize, and hierarchically sequence the most significant attributes or concepts of a topic.
- Serves as a springboard for topic discussions, vocabulary development, summarization, and content review.
- Provides a simple-to-prepare activity that connects to a myriad of topics, content areas, and skills.
- Promotes students' application, analysis, and synthesis.
- Encourages students to list resources as they acquire and organize information.
- Serves as an assessment tool to assess accuracy, depth, and complexity of content.

The Important Thing is a learning experience based upon *The Important Book* by Margaret Wise Brown, and uses the pattern of that book's text to prompt students to analyze significant topical attributes. This pattern asks students to state the most important thing about a topic or concept, substantiate the idea with several significant details, and then conclude by restating the most important thing.

Included at the end of this section are three tiers of templates that enable teachers to appropriately match students' capabilities and differentiate the complexity of the learning

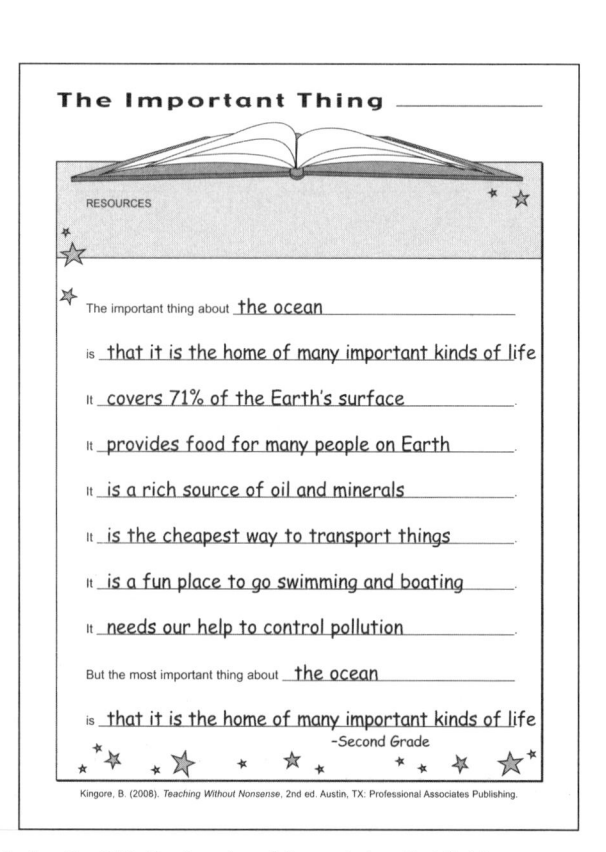

> **The Important Thing**
>
> RESOURCES
>
> The important thing about __the ocean__
> is __that it is the home of many important kinds of life__
> It __covers 71% of the Earth's surface__
> It __provides food for many people on Earth__
> It __is a rich source of oil and minerals__
> It __is the cheapest way to transport things__
> It __is a fun place to go swimming and boating__
> It __needs our help to control pollution__
> But the most important thing about __the ocean__
> is __that it is the home of many important kinds of life__
> –Second Grade
>
> Kingore, B. (2008). *Teaching Without Nonsense*, 2nd ed. Austin, TX: Professional Associates Publishing.

Kingore, B. (2008). *Teaching Without Nonsense*, 2nd ed. Austin, TX: Professional Associates Publishing.

experience. The first template is brief and simple; the second tier requires an expanded analysis with additional attributes; the third tier invites comparative thinking with a more complex syntax. Students and adults can use these examples to develop additional versions that guide students' analysis of content. All three templates use the pronoun *it* when referring to the topic. When a person is used as the subject, the pronoun should be changed appropriately.

Model this learning task with the class to activate their interest. To model an Important Thing format, display a copy of the most appropriate template on the overhead, computer, or chart. Guide the class to brainstorm and list the important attributes of the topic under study. Then, ask students to analyze and rank the significance of the things they have listed. Discussion and negotiation become critical in completing this process and further serve to help students integrate information about the topic. Once the prioritizing is established, the information is elaborated and organized on the Important Thing format. Challenge students to use more advanced and content-specific vocabulary when appropriate.

As a closure, ask students to identify what they enjoyed or did well during this process. Then, discuss together how the class used each of the following skills as they worked to complete the task.

- Recalling information
- Analyzing
- Ranking or prioritizing
- Decision making
- Synthesizing

Applications

Teachers successfully apply the Important Thing formats to multiple content areas and topics. The following list may prompt thinking of applications useful in instruction.

Affective Domain
- Me
- Special events
- Families
- Group building: The Important Things about Our Class

Language Arts
- Character analysis, descriptions, or traits
- Book or story summary
- Main idea and details
- Prewriting activity to then elaborate and expand into a paragraph or longer written response

Kingore, B. (2008). *Teaching Without Nonsense*, 2nd ed. Austin, TX: Professional Associates Publishing.

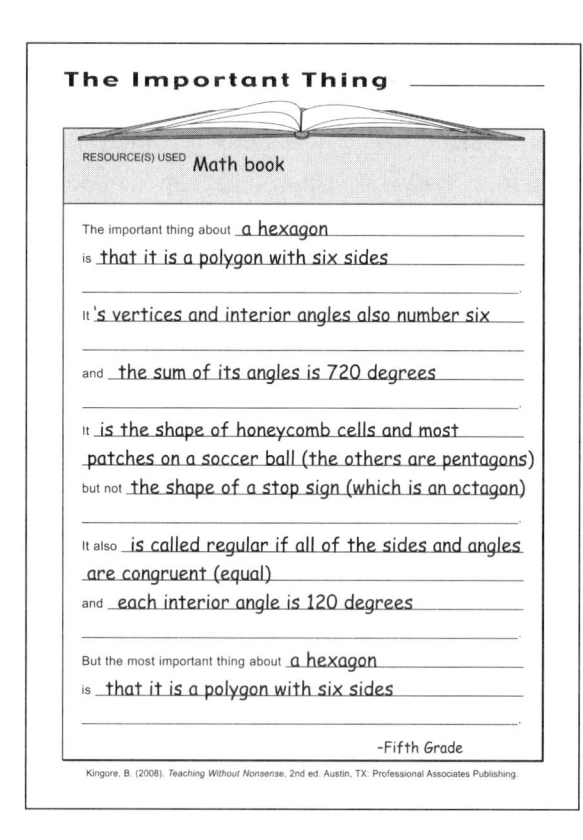

> **The Important Thing** ─────
>
> RESOURCE(S) USED **Math book**
>
> The important thing about **a hexagon**
> is **that it is a polygon with six sides**
>
> It **'s vertices and interior angles also number six**
>
> and **the sum of its angles is 720 degrees**
>
> It **is the shape of honeycomb cells and most patches on a soccer ball (the others are pentagons)**
> but not **the shape of a stop sign (which is an octagon)**
>
> It also **is called regular if all of the sides and angles are congruent (equal)**
> and **each interior angle is 120 degrees**
>
> But the most important thing about **a hexagon**
> is **that it is a polygon with six sides**
>
> *-Fifth Grade*
>
> Kingore, B. (2008). *Teaching Without Nonsense*, 2nd ed. Austin, TX: Professional Associates Publishing.

Math
- Problem solving
- Math strategy or process analysis
- Attributes of geometric shapes
- Analysis of math operations

Science
- Attributes of animals, insects, and birds
- Scientific method
- Analytical review of an experiment
- Summary of a science topic
- Environments

Social Studies
- Attributes of capitals, regions, states, or countries
- Historical people, places, and events
- Patriotic symbols
- Social or cultural mores

Variations

- Promote depth and complexity by requiring students to record their sources of information. Teachers find that students' responses use more specific information and vocabulary when encouraged to incorporate multiple resources.

- Eventually, many students use and complete these formats without direct teacher instruction. At that point, the formats provide an effective product for students to use to report the results of their research and individual study.

- Challenge students to use one of the tiers to develop a summary for the current topic of study. Students then jigsaw their information with other students in a small group.

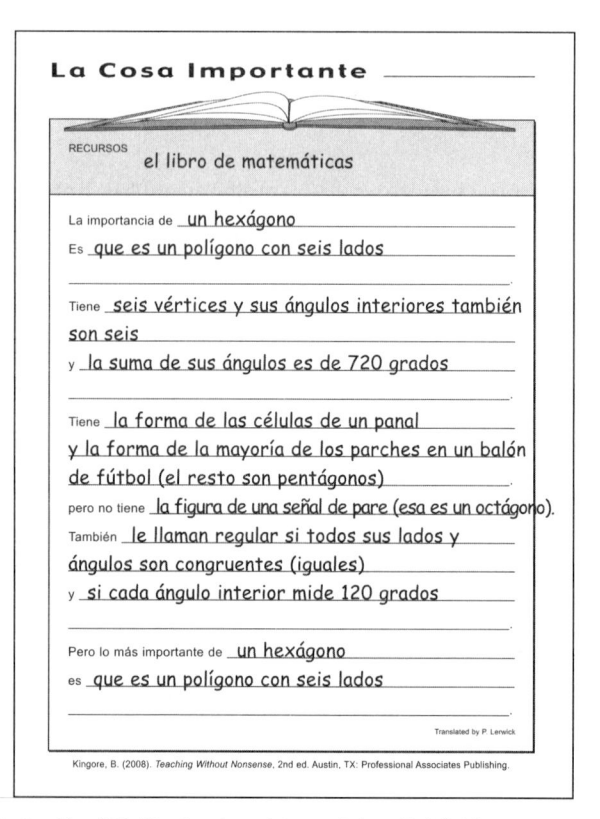

> **La Cosa Importante** ─────
>
> RECURSOS **el libro de matemáticas**
>
> La importancia de **un hexágono**
> Es **que es un polígono con seis lados**
>
> Tiene **seis vértices y sus ángulos interiores también son seis**
> y **la suma de sus ángulos es de 720 grados**
>
> Tiene **la forma de las células de un panal y la forma de la mayoría de los parches en un balón de fútbol (el resto son pentágonos)**
> pero no tiene **la figura de una señal de pare (esa es un octágono)**.
> También **le llaman regular si todos sus lados y ángulos son congruentes (iguales)**
> y **si cada ángulo interior mide 120 grados**
>
> Pero lo más importante de **un hexágono**
> es **que es un polígono con seis lados**
>
> *Translated by P. Lenwick*
>
> Kingore, B. (2008). *Teaching Without Nonsense*, 2nd ed. Austin, TX: Professional Associates Publishing.

Kingore, B. (2008). *Teaching Without Nonsense*, 2nd ed. Austin, TX: Professional Associates Publishing.

SECTION 2: Learning Experiences

- To prompt more abstract thinking, greater complexity, and depth in students' analysis and search for information, designate specific aspects of a topic that students must incorporate in their responses. For example, label each line of the template with a concept or skill students must demonstrate through their content on that line. Concepts, such as *perspective, terminology, issue,* and *change over time* are effective prompts to tease out high-level thinking and complexity.

Options for Implementation

Evaluation Tool

> **The Important Thing**
>
> RESOURCE: *Seven Blind Mice* by Ed Young
>
> The important thing about _Seven Blind Mice_
> is _that it is a good story_.
> It _has mice finding Elephant parts_.
> It _uses colors, numbers, and days_.
> It _is a little funny_.
> But the most important thing about _Seven Blind Mice_
> is _that it is a good story to read_.
> —First Grade
>
> Kingore, B. (2008). *Teaching Without Nonsense*, 2nd ed. Austin, TX: Professional Associates Publishing.

Use the appropriate tier of Important Thing as a culminating product to evaluate students' understanding and application of the most significant points of the current topic of study. Share a rubric with the class before they begin the task so they understand the intended evaluation criteria. The rubric clarifies the standard for grading and goes beyond judging only correct or incorrect to document the depth and complexity of the different responses. Similar to the rubrics for open-ended products included in the first section of this book, relevant criteria could include information depth, vocabulary, organization, level of thinking, and/or written conventions.

Kingore, B. (2008). *Teaching Without Nonsense*, 2nd ed. Austin, TX: Professional Associates Publishing.

Important Thing Tiering Chart

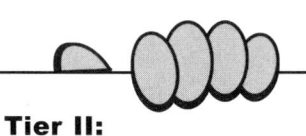

Tier I: Simpler Applications	Tier II: More Complex Applications
The teacher facilitates or pairs of students work together for support.	Individuals complete a mid-level response demonstrating depth and complexity.
The response is in words or phrases.	The response is in sentences and incorporates content that is more abstract or complex.
The vocabulary is accurate but basic.	The vocabulary is more complex with multi-syllable, topic specific words.
Students use the simple template to develop a response individually or in small groups.	Individuals or pairs of students use the middle or complex-level template to develop a response that incorporates the specific concepts designated for each line.
The content or topic is simple but accurate.	Individuals or pairs of students use the most complex template to develop a response using above grade-level resources.
Students use the mid-level template to develop a response individually or in small groups. The response reflects grade-level resources, information, and vocabulary.	Individual students use the most complex template to develop a response to summarize their research. They use beyond grade-level resources, advanced vocabulary, and organize more complex, abstract information.

Kingore, B. (2008). *Teaching Without Nonsense*, 2nd ed. Austin, TX: Professional Associates Publishing.

The Important Thing

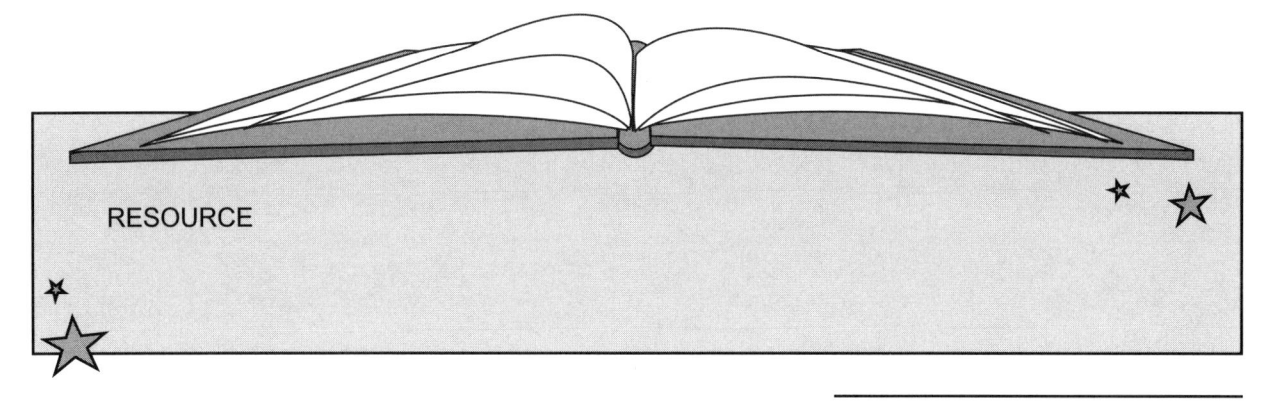

RESOURCE

The important thing about _____

is _____.

It _____.

It _____.

It _____.

But the most important thing about _____

is _____.

Kingore, B. (2008). *Teaching Without Nonsense*, 2nd ed. Austin, TX: Professional Associates Publishing.

La Cosa Importante

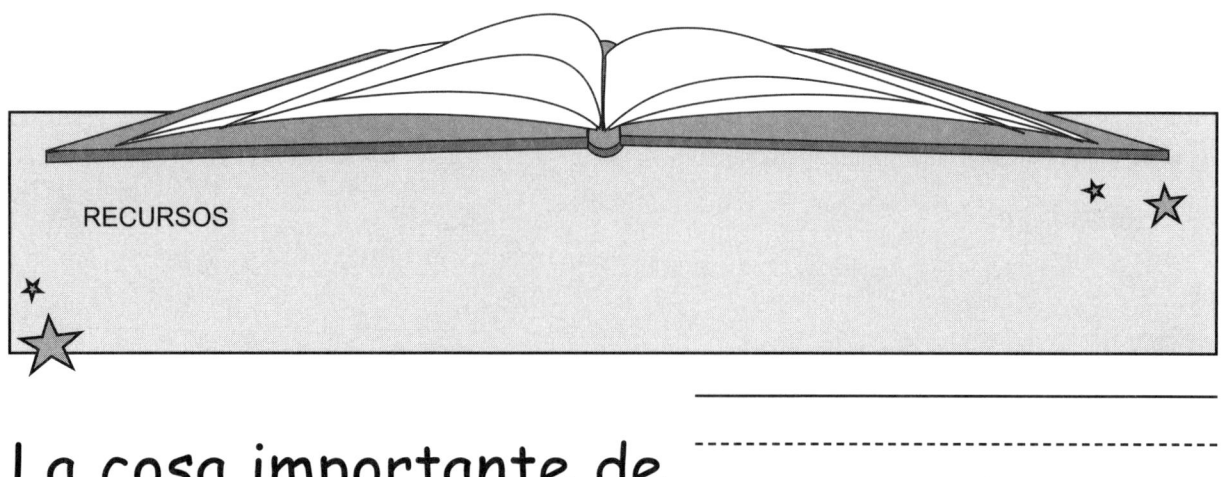

RECURSOS

La cosa importante de _____

es _____.

Es _____.

Es _____.

Es _____.

Pero la cosa importante de _____

es _____.

Translated by P. Lerwick

Kingore, B. (2008). *Teaching Without Nonsense*, 2nd ed. Austin, TX: Professional Associates Publishing.

The Important Thing

RESOURCES

The important thing about _____

is _____.

It _____.

It _____.

It _____.

It _____.

It _____.

It _____.

But the most important thing about _____

is _____.

Kingore, B. (2008). *Teaching Without Nonsense*, 2nd ed. Austin, TX: Professional Associates Publishing.

La Cosa Importante _____

RECURSOS

La cosa importante de _____

es _____.

Es _____.

Es _____.

Es _____.

Es _____.

Es _____.

Es _____.

Pero la cosa importante de _____

es _____.

Translated by P. Lerwick

Kingore, B. (2008). *Teaching Without Nonsense*, 2nd ed. Austin, TX: Professional Associates Publishing.

The Important Thing _____

RESOURCES

The important thing about _____

is _____

_____.

It _____

_____

and _____

_____.

It _____

_____

but not _____

_____.

It also _____

_____

and _____

_____.

But the most important thing about _____

is _____

_____.

Kingore, B. (2008). *Teaching Without Nonsense*, 2nd ed. Austin, TX: Professional Associates Publishing.

La Cosa Importante _____

RECURSOS

La importancia de _____

Es _____
_____.

Tiene _____
_____

y _____
_____.

Tiene _____
_____
_____.

pero no tiene _____

También _____
_____

y _____
_____.

Pero lo más importante de _____

es _____
_____.

Translated by P. Lerwick

Kingore, B. (2008). *Teaching Without Nonsense*, 2nd ed. Austin, TX: Professional Associates Publishing.

Scavenger Hunt

Grade Levels: K-8

Beginning reading skills are required in order for kindergartners to complete scavenger hunts.

A scavenger hunt learning experience:
- Promotes the recall and review of information
- Promotes the practice and extension of skills
- Serves as a springboard for applying, discussing, and extending a variety of skills and concepts related to a topic of study
- Serves as an assessment tool to assess students' integration and transfer of skills

A scavenger hunt learning experience is a variation of the popular activity that involves students moving about to retrieve designated items. This variation can be kinesthetic to invite whole-body movement or be stationary to require less activity and entice students to apply basic skills and concepts through motivating forms of print (other than a text book). Print resources for stationary scavenger hunts include menus, telephone books, cereal boxes, comic strips, television program guide, poems, familiar songs, and newspapers. Using the included planning form, determine which print and materials to use, select which skills or concepts to incorporate, and plan several scavenger tasks for the students.

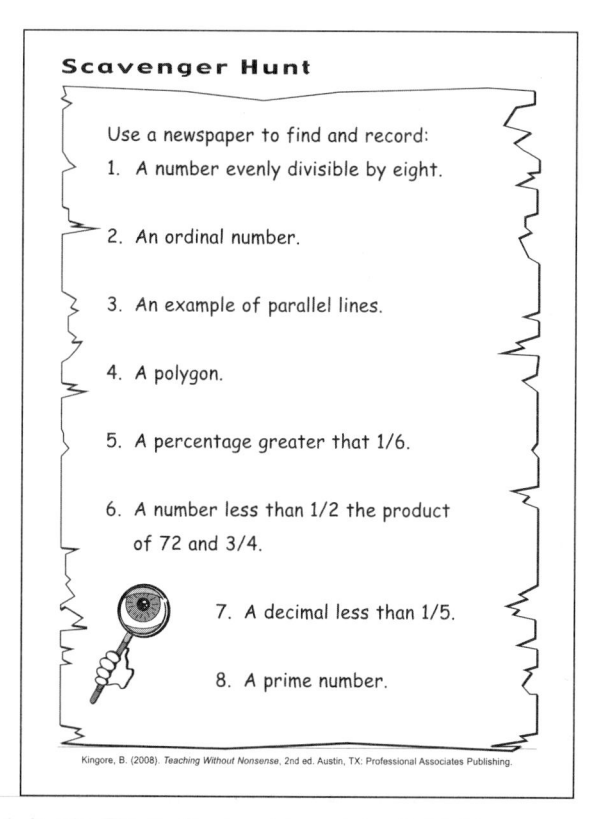

> **Scavenger Hunt**
>
> Use a newspaper to find and record:
> 1. A number evenly divisible by eight.
> 2. An ordinal number.
> 3. An example of parallel lines.
> 4. A polygon.
> 5. A percentage greater that 1/6.
> 6. A number less than 1/2 the product of 72 and 3/4.
> 7. A decimal less than 1/5.
> 8. A prime number.
>
> Kingore, B. (2008). *Teaching Without Nonsense*, 2nd ed. Austin, TX: Professional Associates Publishing.

Kingore, B. (2008). *Teaching Without Nonsense*, 2nd ed. Austin, TX: Professional Associates Publishing.

Scavenger Hunt

GRADE LEVEL _____   MATERIALS _____

_____

List the skills to incorporate or extend.

Write several tasks that apply those skills.

Kingore, B. (2008). *Teaching Without Nonsense*, 2nd ed. Austin, TX: Professional Associates Publishing.

Scavenger Hunt

GRADE LEVEL _____   MATERIALS _____

_____

List the skills to incorporate or extend.

Write several tasks that apply those skills.

Kingore, B. (2008). *Teaching Without Nonsense*, 2nd ed. Austin, TX: Professional Associates Publishing.

Variations

Kinesthetic Scavenger Hunt

A kinesthetic scavenger hunt invites students to move about the classroom to find targeted information. This learning experience is welcomed by kinesthetic learners, involves students interacting and exchanging information, and helps build a community of learners in a classroom by enabling students to talk and learn from one another.

To model a kinesthetic scavenger hunt, use the provided example or prepare a simple version and make copies for each student. Explain that the objective is to work alone or with one other student to find and record all of the information requested on the hunt. Students quietly move around the room using the entire room as a source of information.

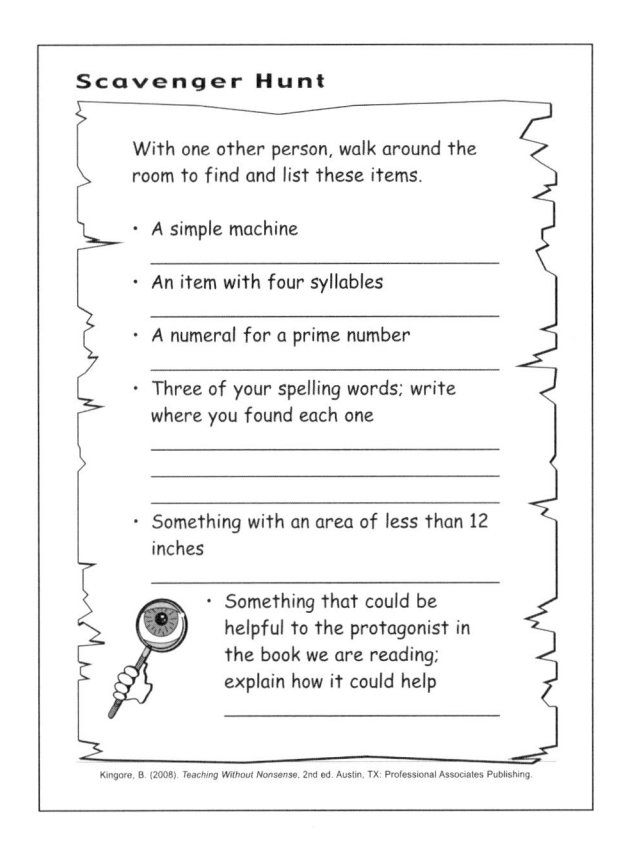

Scavenger Hunt

With one other person, walk around the room to find and list these items.

- A simple machine
- An item with four syllables
- A numeral for a prime number
- Three of your spelling words; write where you found each one
- Something with an area of less than 12 inches
- Something that could be helpful to the protagonist in the book we are reading; explain how it could help

Kingore, B. (2008). *Teaching Without Nonsense*, 2nd ed. Austin, TX: Professional Associates Publishing.

Ask the children to suggest appropriate behaviors so this game will be fun rather than disruptive. Prompt the group to reach decisions about noise levels and safe, sensible movements. When behaviors are agreed upon, begin the hunt. If desired, use a timer to control the length of the search. Come back together for closure to debrief the process and elicit students' suggestions of improvements for the next hunt.

Stationary Scavenger Hunt

A stationary scavenger hunt invites students to scan print to find targeted skills and vocabulary. This learning experience is an engaging way to assess the level at which students are able to apply needed skills.

To model this learning task, use one of the provided examples or prepare a simple scavenger hunt to display on the chalkboard, computer, or chart. Use a form of print that will engage the students, such as a cereal box, menu, or newspaper. Read each scavenger task aloud, and scan the print together to find examples of the designated skill or concept. As students become familiar with the task, have them proceed in pairs to complete the scavenger hunt. For closure, come back together as a whole group to debrief the process and respond to any questions. Invite students to share the strategies they used to complete the task.

Kingore, B. (2008). *Teaching Without Nonsense*, 2nd ed. Austin, TX: Professional Associates Publishing.

With experience, individual students can complete scavenger hunts as independent learning tasks. With young students and students for whom writing is difficult, design scavenger hunts that apply skills using any page from a newspaper. Children use a highlighter to mark the skill examples they find instead of writing responses. When using other print sources, students record their responses on paper.

Student-Produced Scavenger Hunts

- Individuals or small groups work together to create original versions of scavenger hunts for other students to complete. List specific skills and vocabulary words for them to incorporate. Challenge students to elaborate and use more advanced and content specific vocabulary when appropriate.

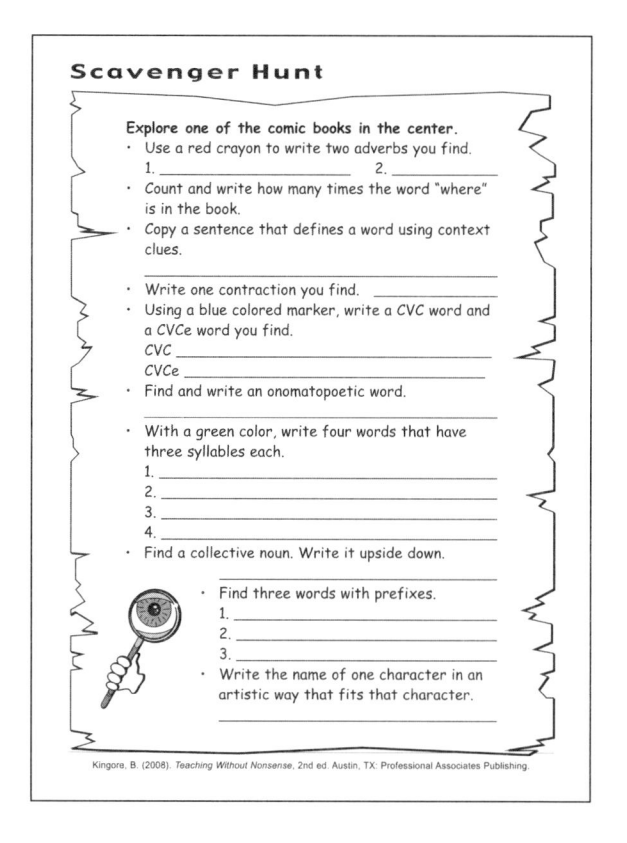

Scavenger Hunt

Explore one of the comic books in the center.
- Use a red crayon to write two adverbs you find.
  1. _____ 2. _____
- Count and write how many times the word "where" is in the book.
- Copy a sentence that defines a word using context clues.
  _____
- Write one contraction you find. _____
- Using a blue colored marker, write a CVC word and a CVCe word you find.
  CVC _____
  CVCe _____
- Find and write an onomatopoetic word.
- With a green color, write four words that have three syllables each.
  1. _____
  2. _____
  3. _____
  4. _____
- Find a collective noun. Write it upside down.
  _____
- Find three words with prefixes.
  1. _____
  2. _____
  3. _____
- Write the name of one character in an artistic way that fits that character.

Kingore, B. (2008). *Teaching Without Nonsense*, 2nd ed. Austin, TX: Professional Associates Publishing.

- As a self-esteem boost and application for students needing more experience with basic skills or even below grade-level skills, invite them to prepare a scavenger hunt for a younger class. List the skills and terminology for them to include, and arrange for the younger class to actually complete the scavenger hunt. Authentic audiences increase students' motivation to excel.

- Challenge students to create scavenger hunts using literary elements or contents from non-fiction books, stories, or novels the class has completed. Each answer could be a significant item in the story, a character, or the title of one book. For example, using *If the World Were a Village* by David Smith invite students to find the current world population, the most common form of government in the world, and the percentage of the world that is the same age as the student.

- ELL students work together to create scavenger hunts using two or more languages. For example, the statements could be written in English and the answers in a second language.

Options for Implementation

- Prepare kinesthetic scavenger hunts to have ready as a change of pace or novelty to rejuvenate the class.

Kingore, B. (2008). *Teaching Without Nonsense*, 2nd ed. Austin, TX: Professional Associates Publishing.

SECTION 2: Learning Experiences

- Provide stationary scavenger hunts as a learning-station task. As the examples in this section demonstrate, skills and concept from multiple content areas are applicable for scavenger hunt tasks. Encourage students to quietly share and compare their results.

- To save preparation time, develop and laminate generalizable scavenger hunts, such as the primary skills example here using the newspaper. Use an overhead pen to write in specific skill examples for children to apply, as in the second example here. In this way, the same generalizable hunt can be used multiple times to incorporate a variety of specific applications.

Scavenger Hunt

Explore one of the menus.
Find the least expensive and most expensive item. How much would you save ordering the cheap item?
Least expensive: _____ Cost: _____
Most expensive: _____ Cost: _____
AMOUNT SAVED: _____

Choose which three things you would most like to eat and compute your cost if you ordered them.
1. _____ Cost: _____
2. _____ Cost: _____
3. _____ Cost: _____
AMOUNT SPENT: _____

Determine the amount of sales tax for your three choices using the current sales tax in your state.

Compute what a 15% tip would add to your total.

What would be your total cost, including tax and tip, if you were taking three other people to dinner for the same price each?

Kingore, B. (2008). *Teaching Without Nonsense*, 2nd ed. Austin, TX: Professional Associates Publishing.

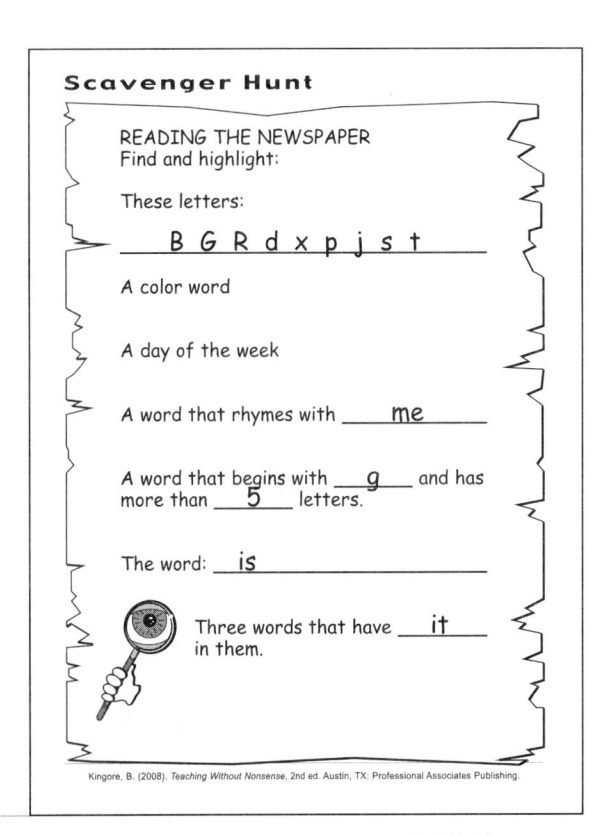

Scavenger Hunt

READING THE NEWSPAPER
Find and highlight:

These letters:
_____

A color word

A day of the week

A word that rhymes with _____

A word that begins with _____ and has more than _____ letters.

The word: _____

Three words that have _____ in them.

Kingore, B. (2008). *Teaching Without Nonsense*, 2nd ed. Austin, TX: Professional Associates Publishing.

Scavenger Hunt

READING THE NEWSPAPER
Find and highlight:

These letters:
B G R d x p j s t

A color word

A day of the week

A word that rhymes with __me__

A word that begins with __g__ and has more than __5__ letters.

The word: __is__

Three words that have __it__ in them.

Kingore, B. (2008). *Teaching Without Nonsense*, 2nd ed. Austin, TX: Professional Associates Publishing.

Kingore, B. (2008). *Teaching Without Nonsense*, 2nd ed. Austin, TX: Professional Associates Publishing.

Scavenger Hunt Tiering Chart

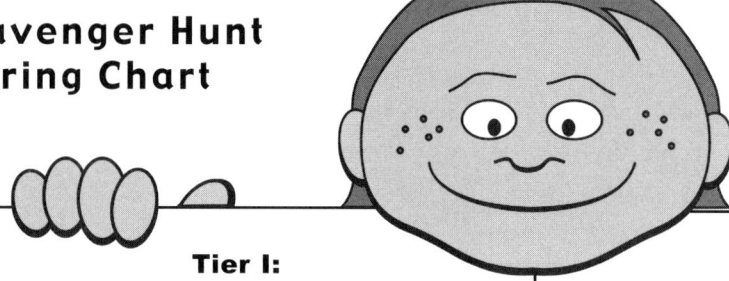

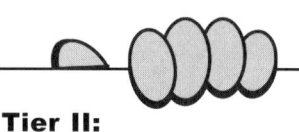

Tier I: Simpler Applications	Tier II: More Complex Applications
The teacher facilitates or pairs of students work together to complete a prepared scavenger hunt.	Individuals or pairs of students complete a more challenging scavenger hunt.
Students work independently to complete a simple scavenger hunt using grade-level skills.	Individuals or pairs of students complete a scavenger hunt applying above-grade-level skills.
With adult support, a small group works together using the template to create a scavenger hunt and develop and answer key for that hunt.	An individual or a pair of students uses the template to create a scavenger hunt and develop an answer key for that hunt.
The product applies grade-level skills and vocabulary.	The product applies more complex, higher-level skills and vocabulary.

Kingore, B. (2008). *Teaching Without Nonsense*, 2nd ed. Austin, TX: Professional Associates Publishing.

SECTION 2: Learning Experiences   111

Scavenger Hunt

Kingore, B. (2008). *Teaching Without Nonsense*, 2nd ed. Austin, TX: Professional Associates Publishing.

Thinking Triangle

Grade Levels: K-12

Beginning writing skills are required in order for kindergartners to complete this task.

A Thinking Triangle learning experience:
- Promotes the review and organization of information.
- Serves as a springboard for summarization, topic discussions, and vocabulary development.
- Encourages students' high-level thinking.
- Assesses students' accuracy, depth, and complexity of content.

A Thinking Triangle is a technique for succinctly retelling and organizing information. The first line has one word, the second line two words, the third line three words, and so on to result in a triangular-shaped response. Limiting the number of words requires students to think first and plan the words they use to communicate information. It invites extensive vocabulary exploration as students consider ways to express their ideas in order to phrase them in the appropriate number of words.

Model the thinking triangle learning experience for a current topic of study. On the board or chart, display the five-line template with investigative words as the descriptors. Ask students to state one-word that identifies the topic (what). As students share an appropriate idea, ask them to think of another one-word response for that same line, and then another one-word

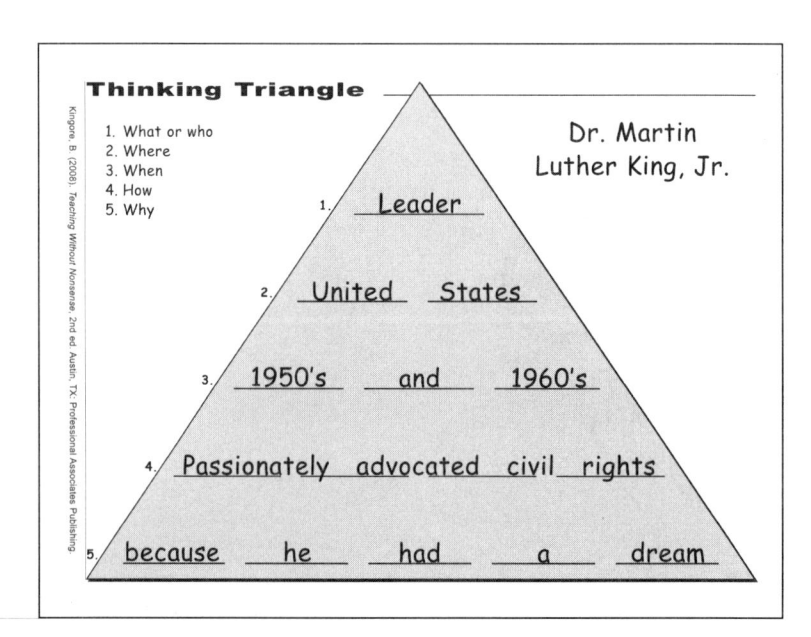

Thinking Triangle

1. What or who
2. Where
3. When
4. How
5. Why

Dr. Martin Luther King, Jr.

1. Leader
2. United States
3. 1950's and 1960's
4. Passionately advocated civil rights
5. because he had a dream

Kingore, B. (2008). *Teaching Without Nonsense*, 2nd ed. Austin, TX: Professional Associates Publishing.

response to model to students that different words can be correct. Ask the group to discuss and select one of the responses. Demonstrate how to organize and record that idea on the first line. Then, proceed in a similar fashion through each of the other lines. When all five lines are complete, ask students to reread the response and determine if there are words they want to change to make the response stronger. Challenge students to use more advanced and content specific vocabulary when appropriate.

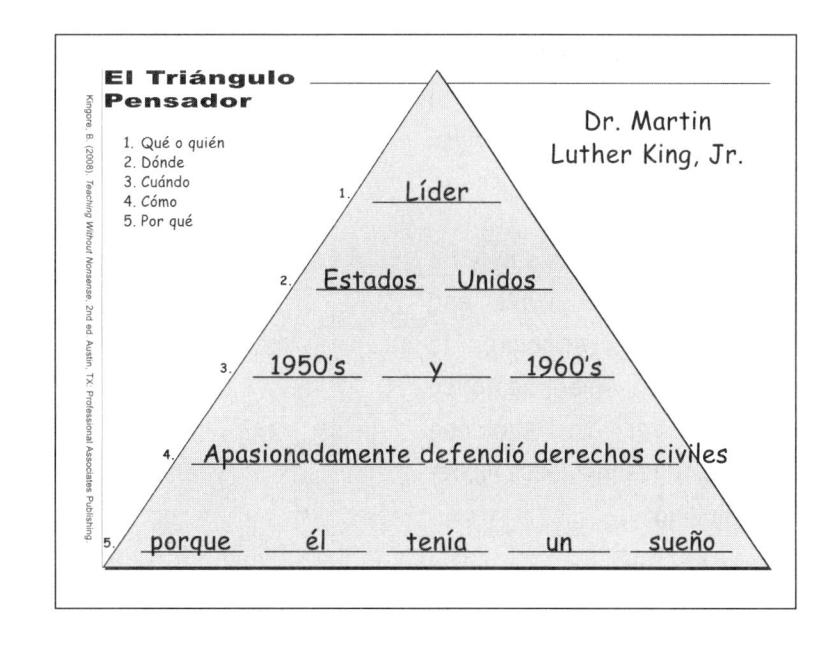

El Triángulo Pensador

1. Qué o quién
2. Dónde
3. Cuándo
4. Cómo
5. Por qué

Dr. Martin Luther King, Jr.

1. Líder
2. Estados Unidos
3. 1950's y 1960's
4. Apasionadamente defendió derechos civiles
5. porque él tenía un sueño

As a closure, sincerely complement the students on their analysis and how effectively they summarized the topic in very few words. Review the process and discuss together how the class used each of the following skills in this process.
- Recalling and organizing information
- Analyzing
- Ranking or prioritizing
- Synthesizing or creating

For additional examples to develop students' experience and confidence in using this learning experience, use the same investigative-words template with other topics. The same template is also an effective choice when summarizing information about an historical figure or person in current events.

Variations

- In pairs or individually, appropriately assign or let students choose the simple, more complex, or most complex version of the Thinking Triangle template to analyze and organize information about assigned topics. Compare the results to substantiate that more than one response can be correct and that different perspectives are possible and valued.

- Investigative words, or wonder words as some primary children like to call them, are simple prompts that apply well to retell literature, people's lives, and events. Use any order for the investigative words, but the learning experience works particularly well when *who* or *what* is used on

Kingore, B. (2008). *Teaching Without Nonsense*, 2nd ed. Austin, TX: Professional Associates Publishing.

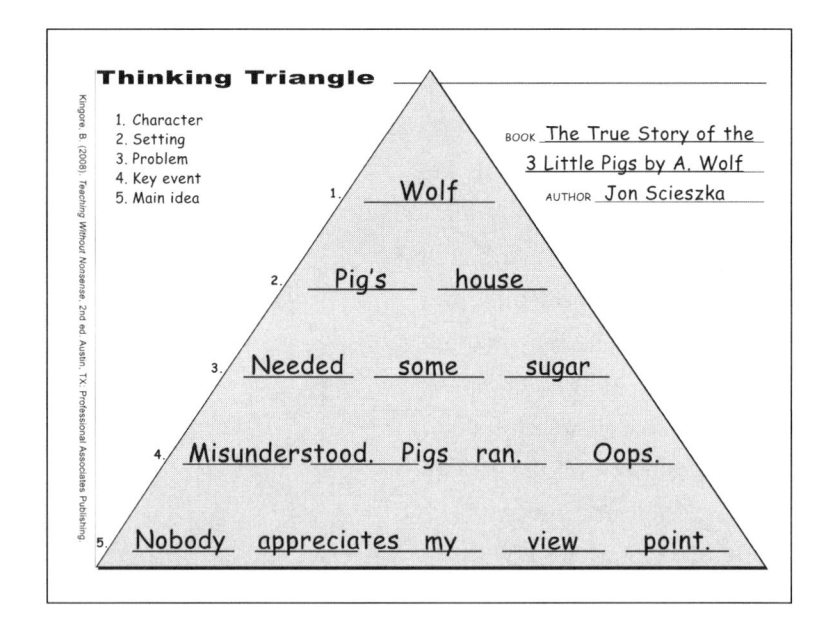

the first line and *why* or *how* are used on the last lines to allow for a bit more elaboration.

Thinking Triangle

1. Character
2. Setting
3. Problem
4. Key event
5. Main idea

BOOK: The True Story of the 3 Little Pigs by A. Wolf
AUTHOR: Jon Scieszka

1. Wolf
2. Pig's house
3. Needed some sugar
4. Misunderstood. Pigs ran. Oops.
5. Nobody appreciates my view point.

- Thinking Triangles may be completed in words and phrases, or structured to require complete-sentence responses. The sentence responses may elicit higher thinking.

- Challenge students to complete two triangles for the same subject, each representing a different point of view. For example, one triangle shares the perspective of Native Americans, and the second triangle presents the perspective of early settlers.

- To increase the potential for complexity and depth in multiple content applications, vary the line prompts and the length of a Thinking Triangle. Using different descriptors, the responses can extend from five to eleven or more lines, depending upon the complexity and depth teachers want students to express. Consider the following three variations as ways to weave together content and high-level thinking. The templates provided at the end of this section trigger additional possibilities.

A. Topic organization and review
1. Topic
2. Significant objects
3. Key words
4. Significant concept
5. The most important point

B. Cause and effect
1. Topic
2. Key words
3. Cause
4. Effect
5. Conclusion

Thinking Triangle

1. Topic
2. Key words
3. Cause
4. Effect
5. Conclusion

1. Learning
2. skills concepts
3. read study think
4. growth self-esteem achievement success
5. Well-planned effort produces life-long learning.

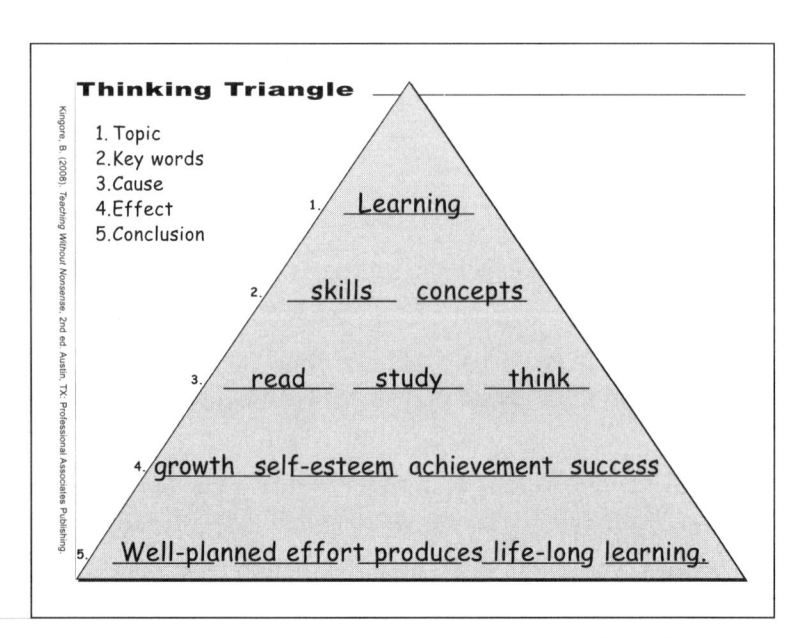

Kingore, B. (2008). *Teaching Without Nonsense*, 2nd ed. Austin, TX: Professional Associates Publishing.

C. Topic, story, person, character, or event analysis
1. Subject
2. When
3. Location
4. Issue or problem
5. Sentence explaining first significant concept, fact, or event
6. Sentence explaining second significant concept, fact, or event
7. Sentence explaining third significant concept, fact, or event
8. Sentence relating the solution, conclusion, or most important point
9. Sentence discussing future trends, personal connection, or personal opinion

- Students can use an eight-line or longer response to organize information gained from their independent study, as the following example for pollution illustrates. Challenge students to develop complex responses that emphasize significant concepts and incorporate advanced and topic-specific vocabulary to demonstrate their understanding.

Thinking Triangle

Kingore, B. (2008). *Teaching Without Nonsense*, 2nd ed. Austin, TX: Professional Associates Publishing.

1. Subject
2. When
3. Location
4. Problem or issue
5. First significant concept, event, or fact
6. Second significant concept, event, or fact
7. Third significant concept, event, or fact
8. Future implications, personal connections, or personal opinions

1. Pollution
2. 21st century
3. U. S. A.
4. Control the environmental decay
5. Environmental Protection Agency regulates emissions.
6. Clean Air Act established air-quality standards.
7. Pollutants in industrial emissions must be reduced.
8. Humans' environmental neglect reflects our apathy and arrogance.

RESOURCE(S) www.epa.gov, Dr. Neidert at WSU, and *Living in the Environment* by G. Miller

Options for Implementation

- On chart paper, copy the five-line template using the investigative words. Laminate the blank template so it can be used multiple times with minimal preparation. When young students enter the classroom eager to talk about an event, such as a fire in the neighborhood, work together using the Thinking Triangle to organize their information. This application honors their interests and allows the class to return to the scheduled curriculum in a timely fashion. When desired, revisit and read the chart as a class literacy experience.

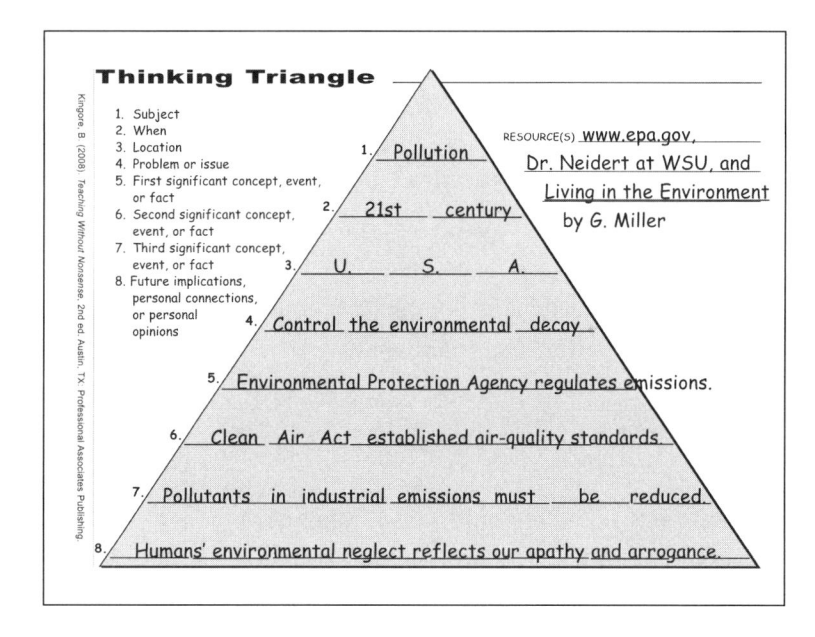

Kingore, B. (2008). *Teaching Without Nonsense*, 2nd ed. Austin, TX: Professional Associates Publishing.

Thinking Triangle Tiering Chart

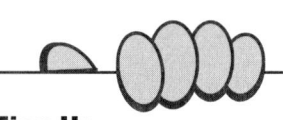

Tier I: Simpler Applications	Tier II: More Complex Applications
The teacher facilitates as students work together to complete the task.	Students work individually to complete Thinking Triangles with contrasting perspectives, such as views from two political candidates.
The response is completed with words or phrases.	The response incorporates sentences requiring analysis and organization.
The content or topic is simple.	The content or topic is more abstract or complex.
The vocabulary is accurate but basic.	The vocabulary is more complex and applies multi-syllable words that are topic specific.
Students individually complete a simple Thinking Triangle.	To document greater depth, students individually complete a longer, more complex, grade-level response incorporating sentences and grade-level vocabulary.
Students complete grade-level responses in small groups. The groups then compare and contrast results.	Individuals or pairs of students develop a longer response using above-grade-level resources and more complex concepts.
Students individually complete a grade-level response. The response is written in sentences and incorporates grade-level vocabulary.	Individual students develop a longer response to summarize their research. They use beyond grade-level resources, apply vocabulary specific to the field, and incorporate complex, abstract information.

Kingore, B. (2008). *Teaching Without Nonsense*, 2nd ed. Austin, TX: Professional Associates Publishing.

SECTION 2: Learning Experiences　　　　　　　　　　　　　　　　　　　　　　　117

Thinking Triangle

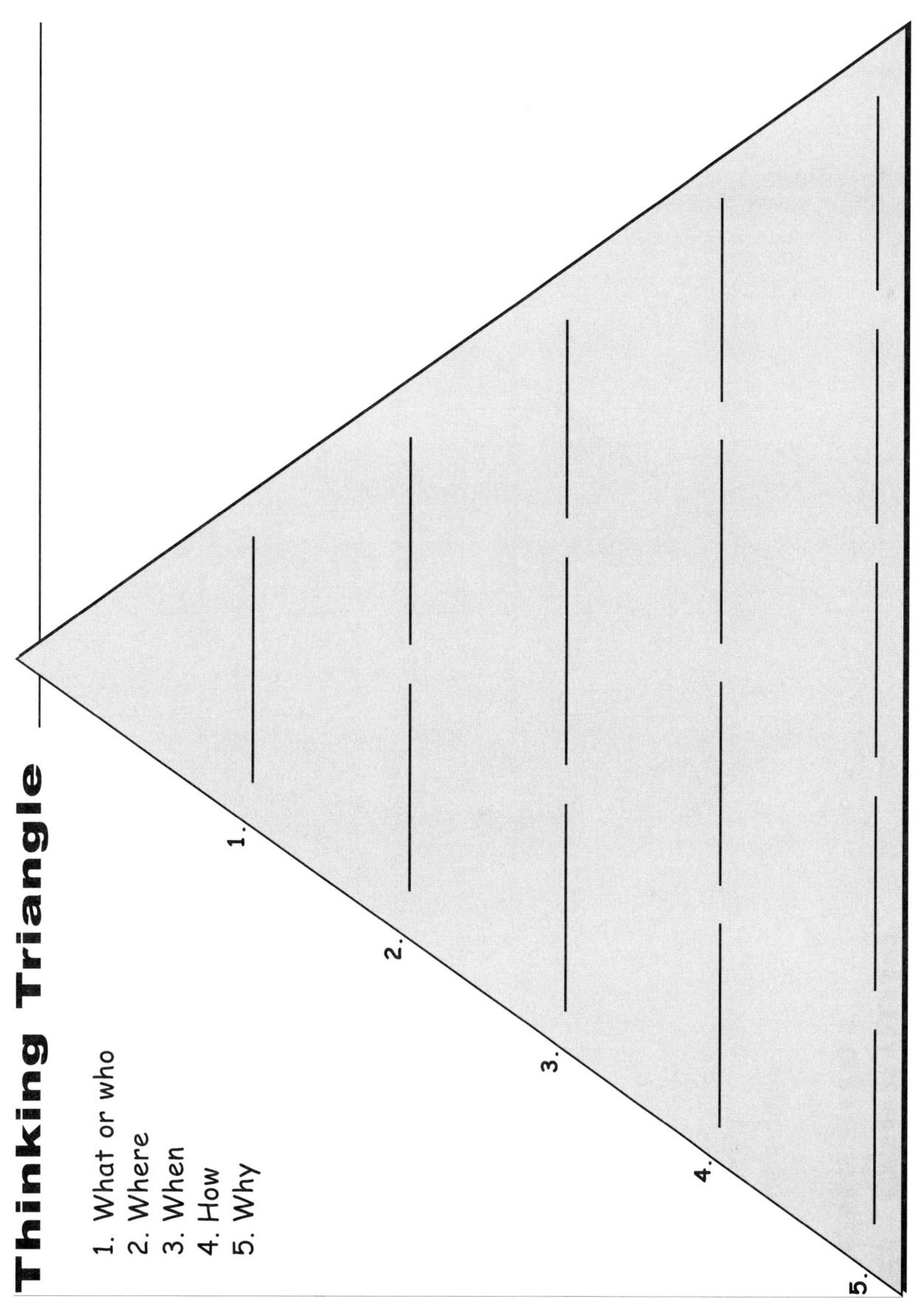

1. What or who
2. Where
3. When
4. How
5. Why

1.
2.
3.
4.
5.

Kingore, B. (2008). *Teaching Without Nonsense*, 2nd ed. Austin, TX: Professional Associates Publishing.

El Triángulo Pensador

1. Qué o quién
2. Dónde
3. Cuándo
4. Cómo
5. Por qué

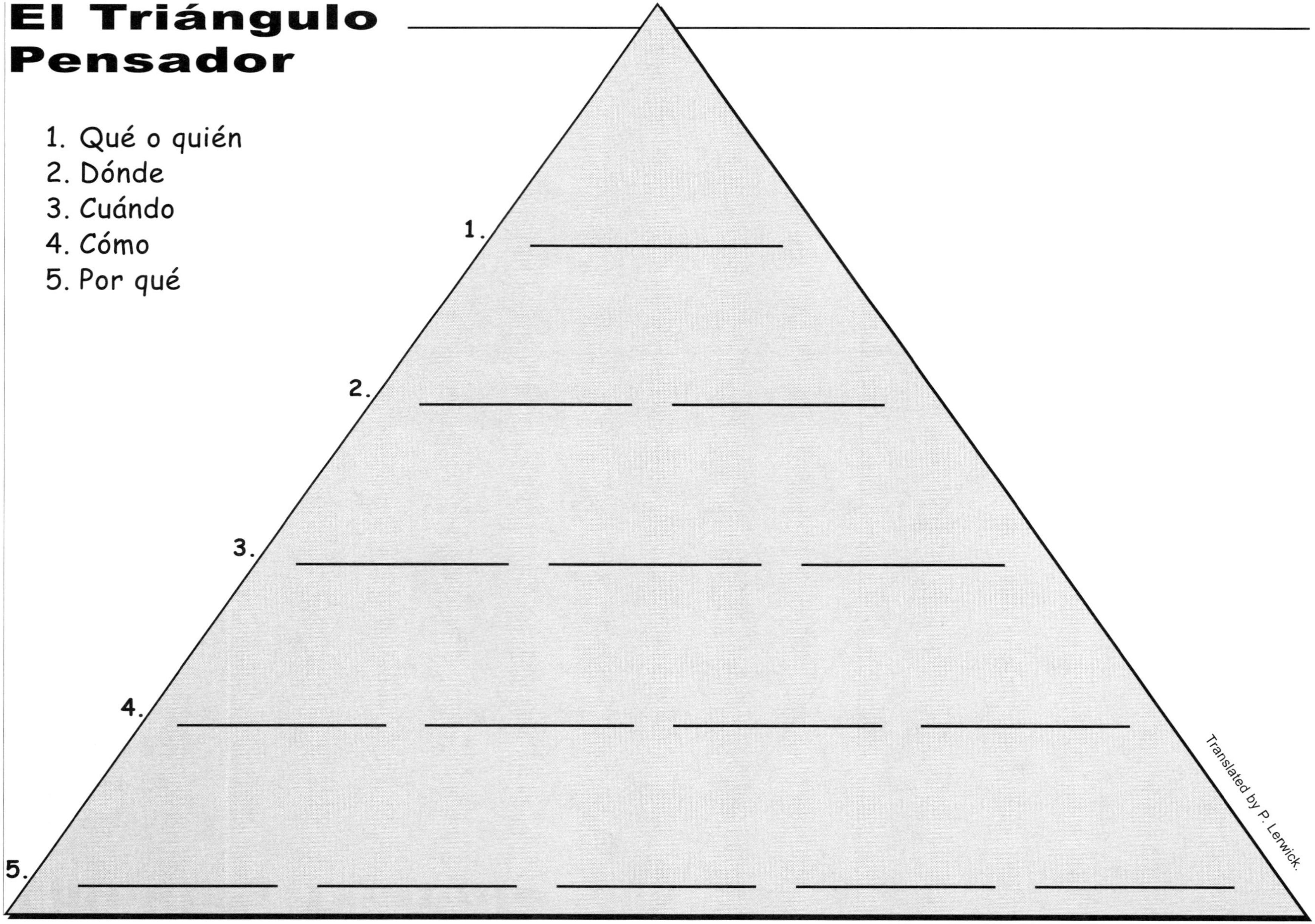

Translated by P. Lerwick.

Kingore, B. (2008). *Teaching Without Nonsense*, 2nd ed. Austin, TX: Professional Associates Publishing.

SECTION 2: Learning Experiences 119

Thinking Triangle

1. Character
2. Setting
3. Problem
4. Key event
5. Main idea

BOOK ―――――
AUTHOR ―――――

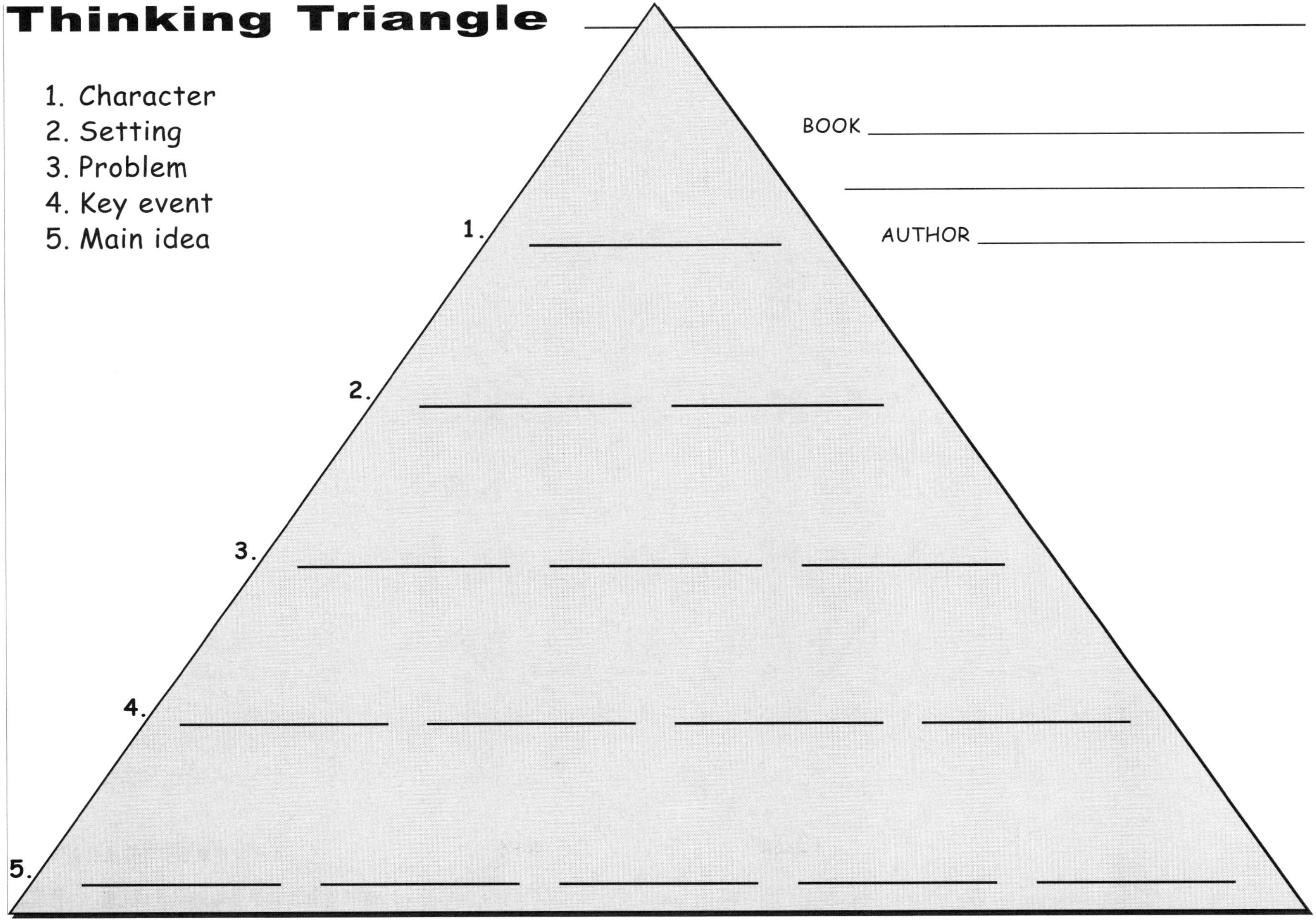

Kingore, B. (2008). *Teaching Without Nonsense*, 2nd ed. Austin, TX: Professional Associates Publishing.

El Triángulo Pensador

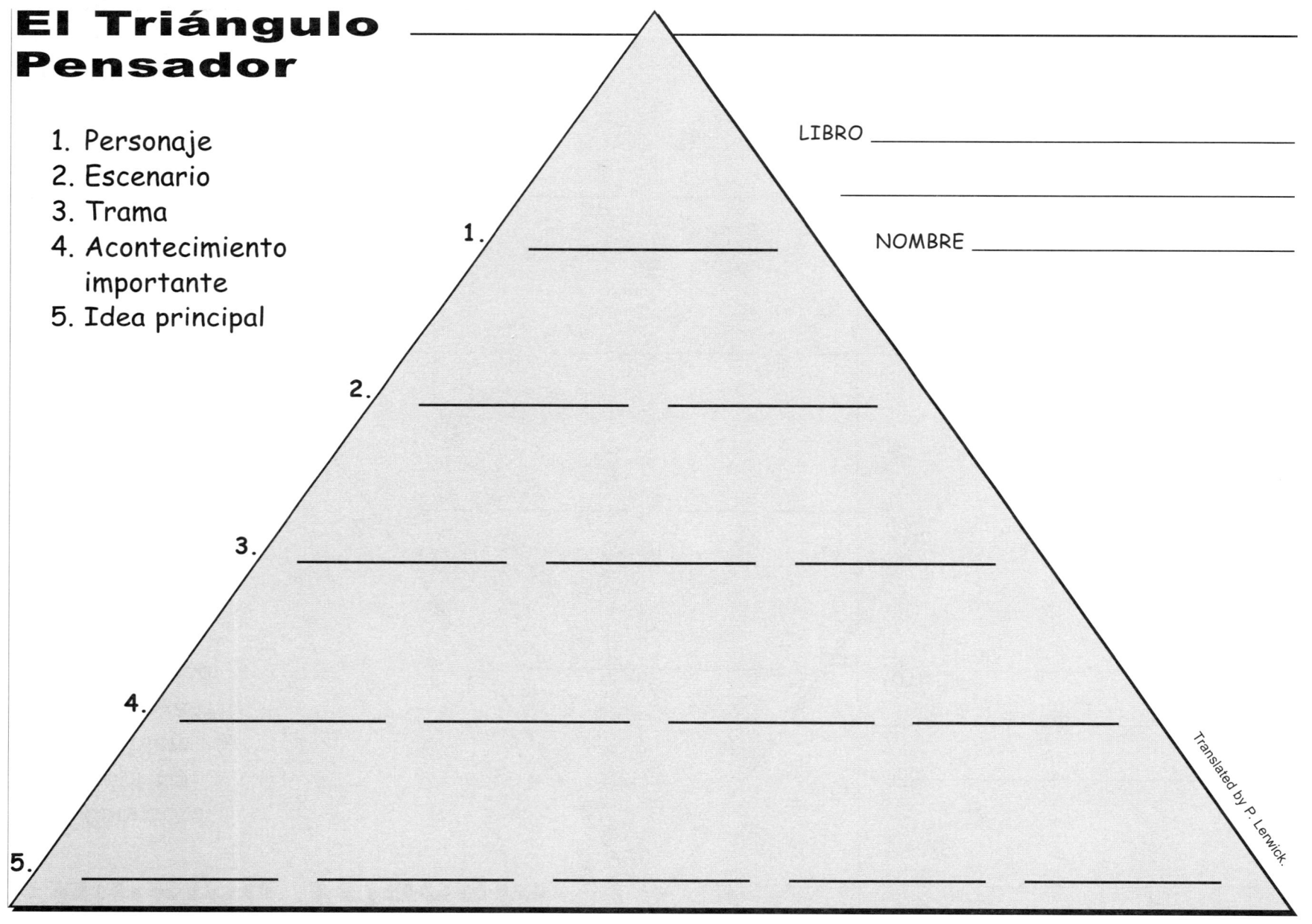

1. Personaje
2. Escenario
3. Trama
4. Acontecimiento importante
5. Idea principal

LIBRO _____
NOMBRE _____

Translated by P. Lerwick.

1.
2.
3.
4.
5.

Kingore, B. (2008). *Teaching Without Nonsense*, 2nd ed. Austin, TX: Professional Associates Publishing.

SECTION 2: Learning Experiences

Thinking Triangle

1. Subject
2. Location
3. Problem
4. Key event
5. Conclusion

RESOURCES _____

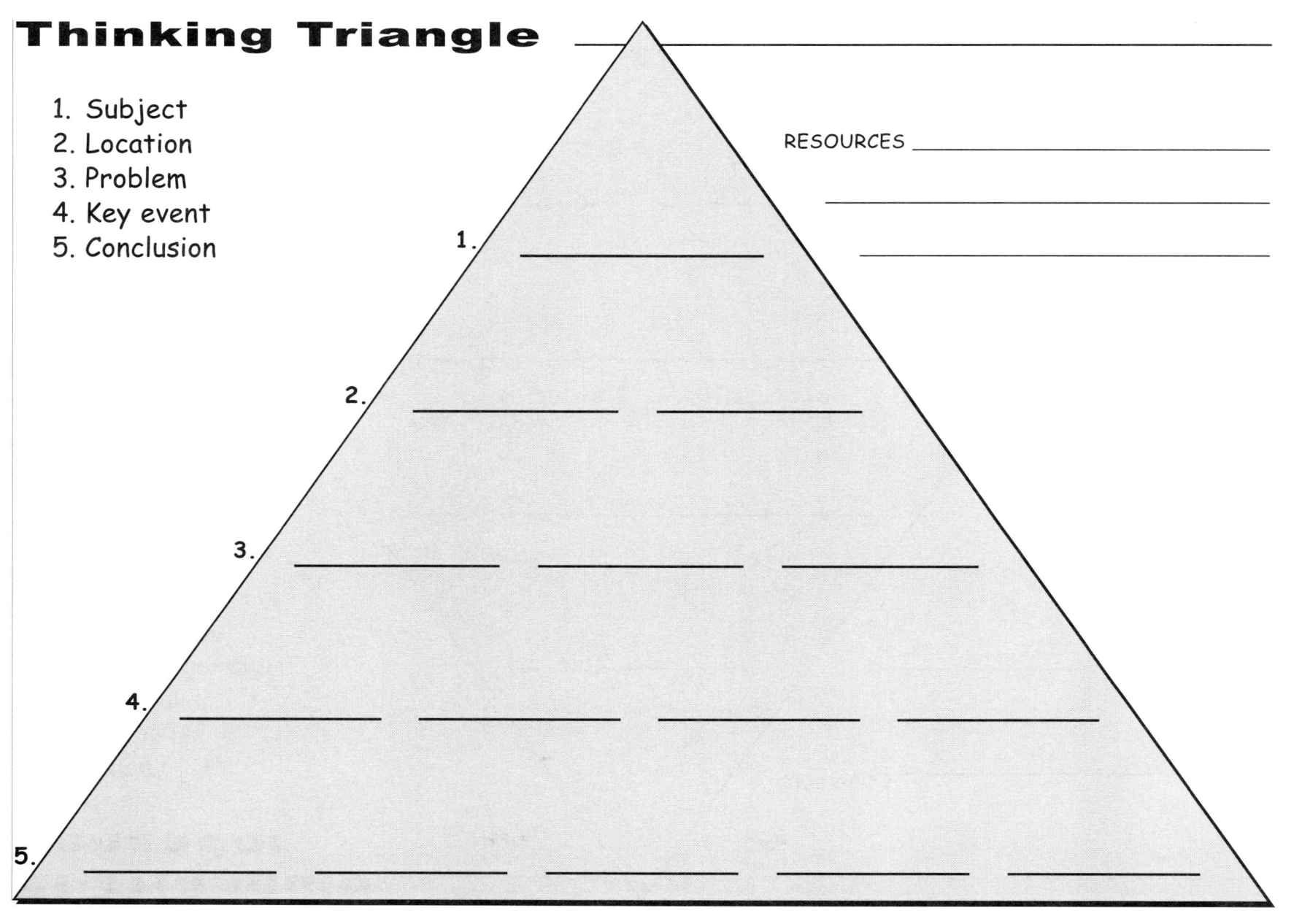

Kingore, B. (2008). *Teaching Without Nonsense*, 2nd ed. Austin, TX: Professional Associates Publishing.

El Triángulo Pensador

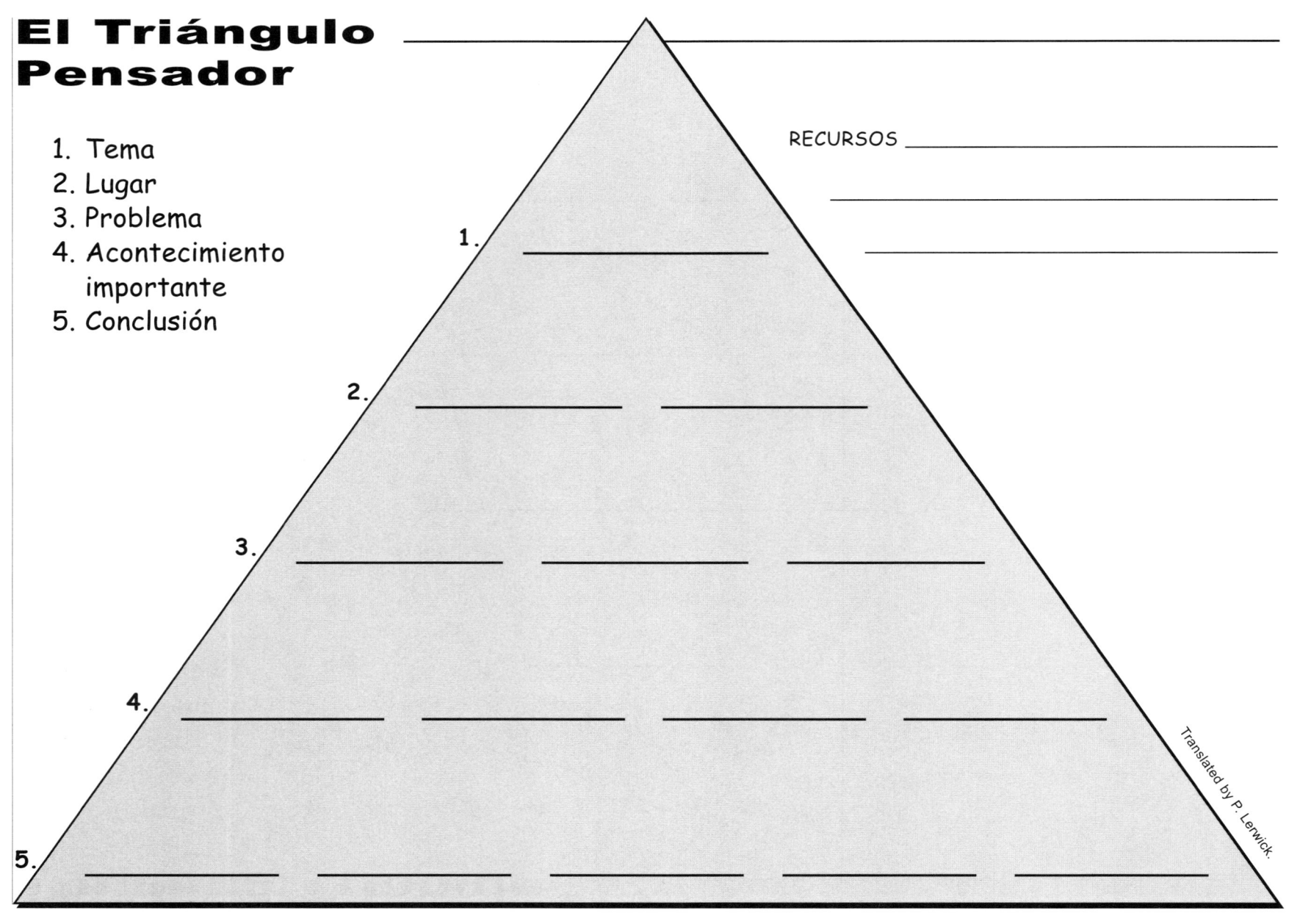

1. Tema
2. Lugar
3. Problema
4. Acontecimiento importante
5. Conclusión

RECURSOS

Translated by P. Lerwick.

Kingore, B. (2008). *Teaching Without Nonsense*, 2nd ed. Austin, TX: Professional Associates Publishing.

SECTION 2: Learning Experiences 123

Thinking Triangle

1. Subject
2. When
3. Location
4. Problem or issue
5. First significant concept, event, or fact
6. Second significant concept, event, or fact
7. Third significant concept, event, or fact
8. Future implications, personal connections, or personal opinions

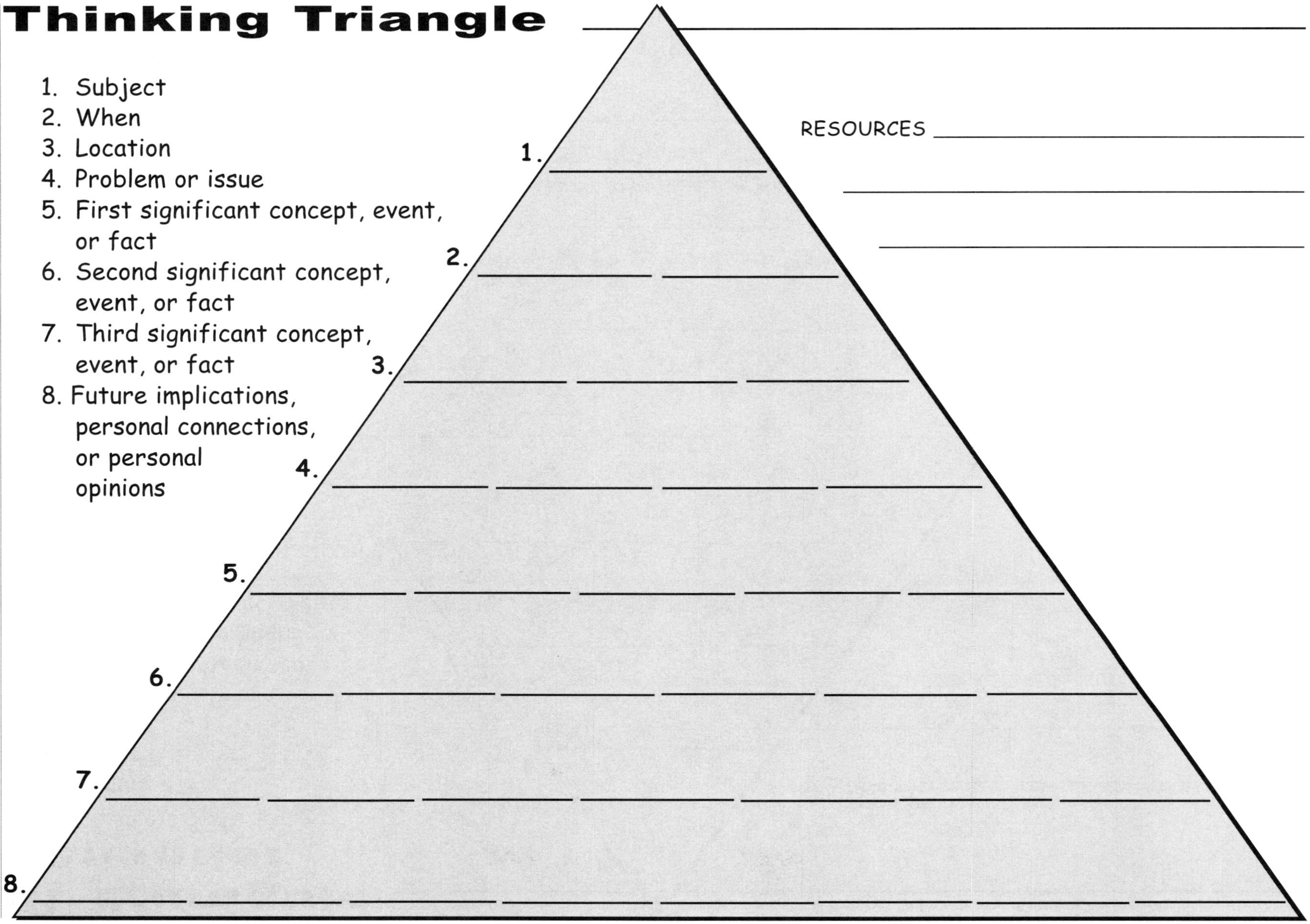

RESOURCES
_____
_____
_____
_____

1.
2.
3.
4.
5.
6.
7.
8.

Kingore, B. (2008). *Teaching Without Nonsense*, 2nd ed. Austin, TX: Professional Associates Publishing.

El Triángulo Pensador

1. Tema
2. Cuándo
3. Lugar
4. Problema o trama
5. Primer acontecimiento significante o hecho
6. Segundo acontecimiento significante o hecho
7. Tercer acontecimiento significante o hecho
8. Implicación en el futuro, conexión personal u opinión personal

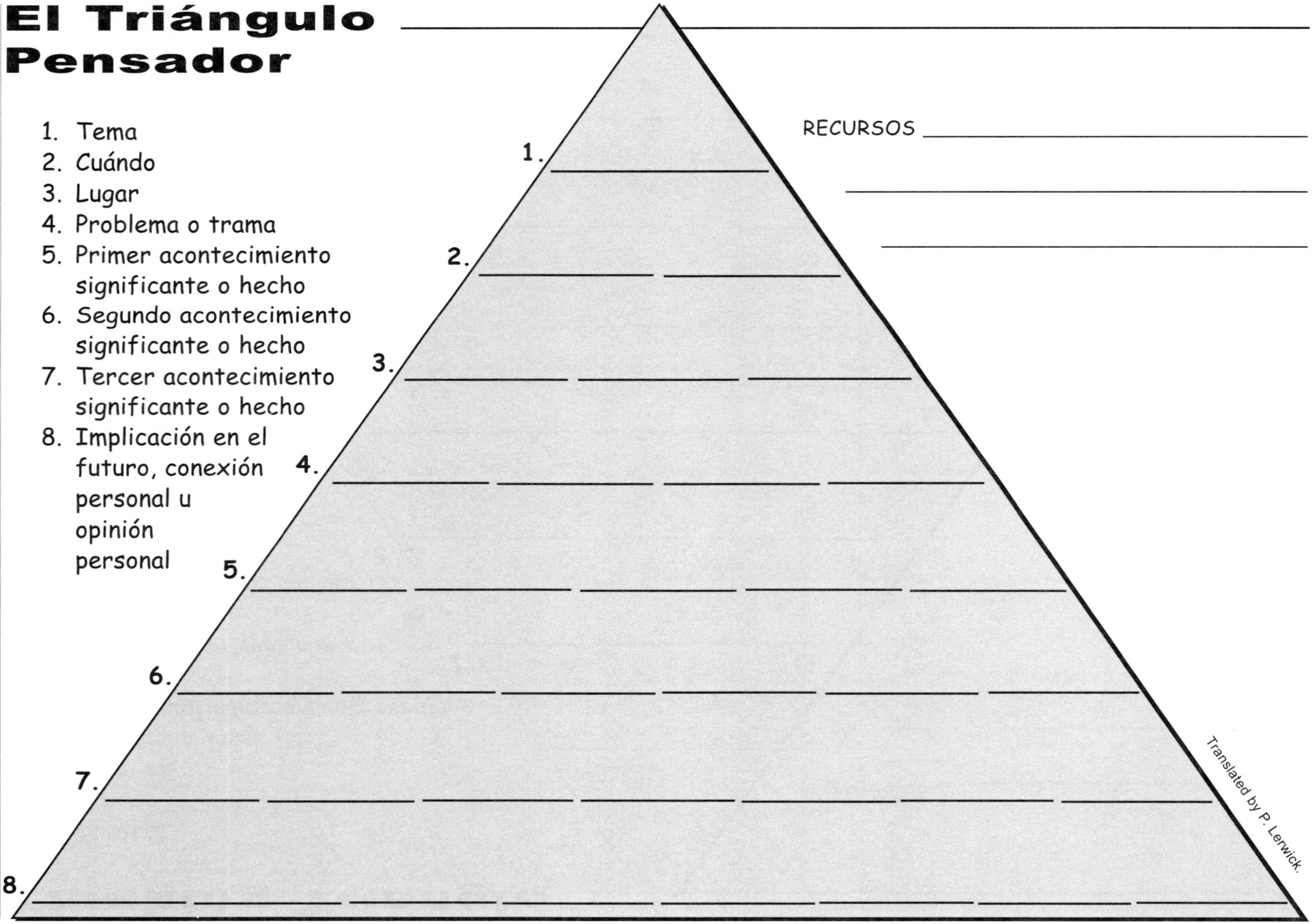

RECURSOS

Translated by P. Lerwick.

Kingore, B. (2008). *Teaching Without Nonsense*, 2nd ed. Austin, TX: Professional Associates Publishing.

Two-Column Chart

Grade Levels: K-8

Kindergartners complete this task with adult facilitation.

The Two-Column Chart is a learning experience that:
- Promotes the review and organization of information for comparative thinking.
- Encourages students to compare and contrast by categorizing and analyzing information.
- Serves as a springboard for topic discussions, vocabulary development, research, and content review.
- Promotes conceptual thinking more than recall or simple thinking.
- Elicits multiple points of view and inference skills.
- Serves as an assessment tool to assess students' accuracy, depth, and complexity of content.

A Two-Column Chart is a learning experience to compare and contrast information about a topic or person. Use the provided chart template or have students simply fold a paper in half to organize areas for recording information. This chart is particularly useful when analyzing any dichotomy.

This chart is quickly understood by students. Typically, modeling one example in front of the class prepares students to use the chart individually for multiple, diverse applications. To model this learning task, display an enlarged copy of the provided chart or fold chart paper in half to designate two areas for

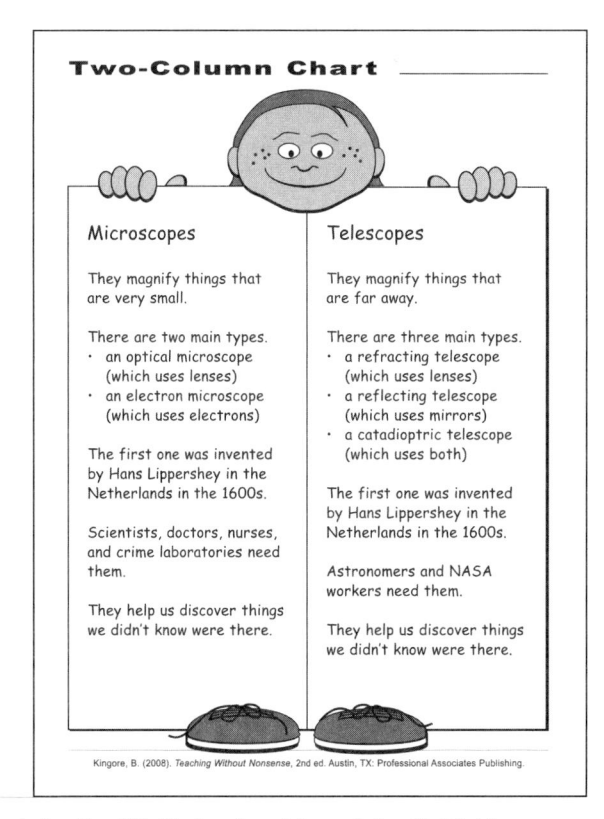

Two-Column Chart

Microscopes	Telescopes
They magnify things that are very small.	They magnify things that are far away.
There are two main types. • an optical microscope (which uses lenses) • an electron microscope (which uses electrons)	There are three main types. • a refracting telescope (which uses lenses) • a reflecting telescope (which uses mirrors) • a catadioptric telescope (which uses both)
The first one was invented by Hans Lippershey in the Netherlands in the 1600s.	The first one was invented by Hans Lippershey in the Netherlands in the 1600s.
Scientists, doctors, nurses, and crime laboratories need them.	Astronomers and NASA workers need them.
They help us discover things we didn't know were there.	They help us discover things we didn't know were there.

Kingore, B. (2008). *Teaching Without Nonsense*, 2nd ed. Austin, TX: Professional Associates Publishing.

organizing data. Label each column with a category that relates to a current topic of study, such as plants and animals, North and South, or items that magnets will and will not attract. Ask the students to suggest ideas and determine where to most appropriately organize each. After several examples are listed for each column, promote students' conceptual thinking by challenging them to reach a conclusion or generalization about the information. As a closure, discuss together how the class uses each of the following skills during this process.

- Recall and organize information
- Compare and contrast
- Form conclusions

Applications

Teachers successfully apply Two-Column Charts to multiple content areas and topics. As one application, with teacher support, young students listed the things that the caterpillar did in *The Very Hungry Caterpillar* by Eric Carle. Then, they researched to compare and contrast what real caterpillars do Their results, shared here, produced lively discussions among the children and motivated them to write a letter to the author to share their information. Some suggestions follow to generate additional creative applications of Two Column Charts.

- Past and present; present and future
- Characters in a book; antagonist versus protagonist
- Predictions before reading and facts after reading
- Easy to do and hard to do (for self-concept and goal setting)
- Opposing political candidates or parties
- Observations and inferences
- Real and fantasy
- Fact and opinion
- Figurative versus literal
- Pro and con for an issue
- Problem and solution
- Cause and effect
- Point of view of different populations
- Two polygons
- Larger and smaller

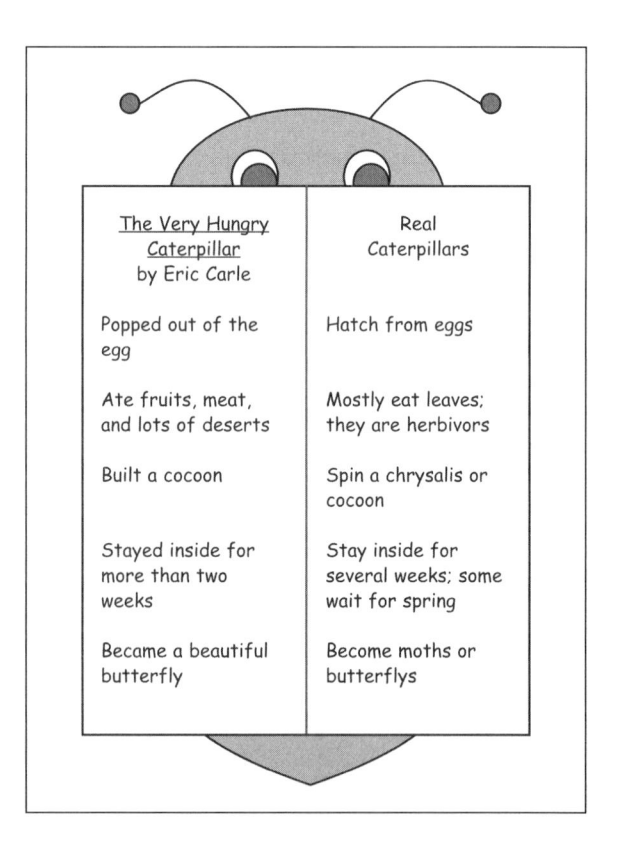

The Very Hungry Caterpillar by Eric Carle	Real Caterpillars
Popped out of the egg	Hatch from eggs
Ate fruits, meat, and lots of deserts	Mostly eat leaves; they are herbivors
Built a cocoon	Spin a chrysalis or cocoon
Stayed inside for more than two weeks	Stay inside for several weeks; some wait for spring
Became a beautiful butterfly	Become moths or butterflys

Kingore, B. (2008). *Teaching Without Nonsense*, 2nd ed. Austin, TX: Professional Associates Publishing.

Variations

- Invite visual-spatial students to create original drawings to illustrate their two-column charts.
- Ask students to fold a paper into three or four columns and label each with a different category. Completing this variation promotes more extensive comparative thinking about the topic.

Options for Implementation

- As an affective task emphasizing change over time as a learner, students use the first column of the chart at the beginning of the year to record information about themselves. Then, students revisit the response at the end of the year to complete the second column with data about themselves at that time. To enhance students' thinking, brainstorm ideas together and generate categories of potential information by suggesting sentence stems, such as this provided list. Add to the visual appeal by inviting students to design the head and feet of the chart to resemble themselves.
    - *I am happy about _____.*
    - *I am always glad to do _____.*
    - *I like _____.*
    - *I am good at _____.*
    - *I think I am not good at _____.*
    - *My personal skills include _____.*
    - *Personally, I would like to change _____.*
    - *My strongest academic skills are in _____.*

- Students use the chart to brainstorm and organize information before writing a comparative piece.

- Small groups of students complete a chart recording facts, inferences, and opinions about opposing sides of a issue. Discuss and clarify together the different nuances of the terms *fact, opinion,* and *inference.* The groups then compare responses to reach a class consensus of the most significant aspects of the issue.

Kingore, B. (2008). *Teaching Without Nonsense,* 2nd ed. Austin, TX: Professional Associates Publishing.

Two-Column Chart
Tiering Chart

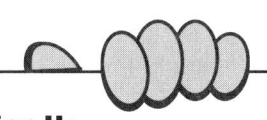

Tier I: Simpler Applications	Tier II: More Complex Applications
The teacher facilitates or pairs of students work together for support.	Individuals complete the chart.
The topic is typical and requires grade-level content.	The topic is more abstract, complex and exceeds typical grade-level content.
The vocabulary is accurate but basic.	The vocabulary is more complex and applies multi-syllable words that are topic specific.
The quantity and quality of the comparisons are adequate.	The quantity of the comparisons is extensive, and the quality is beyond expectations.
	Small groups or individuals conclude the task with a generalization or conclusion about the information.

Kingore, B. (2008). *Teaching Without Nonsense*, 2nd ed. Austin, TX: Professional Associates Publishing.

SECTION 2: Learning Experiences

Two-Column Chart

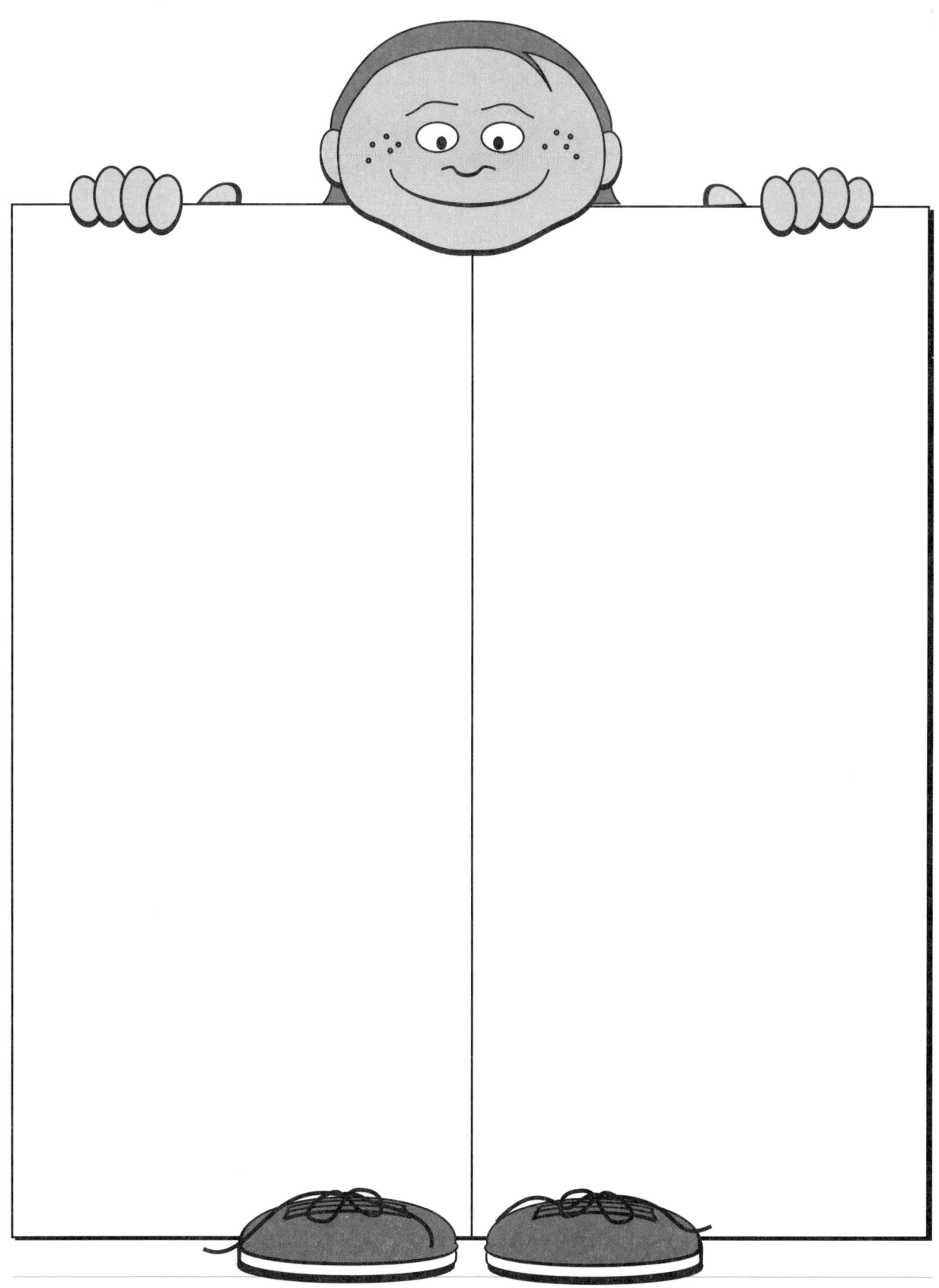

Kingore, B. (2008). *Teaching Without Nonsense*, 2nd ed. Austin, TX: Professional Associates Publishing.

References

Anderson, L. & Krathwohl, D., Eds. (2001). *A taxonomy for learning, teaching, and assessing: A revision of Bloom's taxonomy of educational objectives.* New York: Addison-Wesley Longman.

Association for Supervision and Curriculum Development. (2006). *Building academic vocabulary: Research-based, comprehensive strategies. Research Report.* Alexandria, VA: Author.

Berk, L. & Winsler, Z. (1995). *Scaffolding children's learning: Vygotsky and early childhood education.* Washington, DC: National Association for the Education of Young Children.

Bowie, L. (2007, July 22). *How schools get it right.* The Baltimore Sun. Baltimore, MD.

Bromley, K., Irwin-De Vitis, L., & Modlo, M. (1995). *Graphic Organizers.* New York: Scholastic.

Brown, M. (1949; 1990). *The Important book.* New York: Bantam Doubleday Dell.

Bull, B. & Wittrock, M. (1973). *Imagery in the learning of verbal definitions.* British Journal of Educational Psychology, 43, 289-293.

Caine, R., Caine, G., Klimek, K., & McClintic, C. (2004). *12 Brain/mind learning principles in action.* Thousand Oaks, CA: SAGE Publications.

Carle, E. (1986). *The Very hungry caterpillar.* New York: Scholastic.

Cross, K.P. (1998). Classroom research: Implementing the scholarship of teaching. In T. Angelo (Ed.), *Classroom assessment and research.* (pp. 5-12). San Francisco: Josey-Bass.

Erickson, H. (2007). *Concept-based curriculum and instruction for the thinking classroom.* Thousand Oaks, CA: Corwin Press.

Gardiner, J. (1980). *Stone fox.* New York: Harper & Row.

Grigorenko, E., & Sternberg, R. (1997). *Styles of thinking, abilities, and academic performance.* Exceptional Children, 63, 295-312.

Hertzog, N. (1998). *Open-ended activities: Differentiation through learner responses.* Gifted Child Quarterly, 42, 212-227.

High/Scope Educational Research Foundation. (2005). *Lifetime effects: The High/Scope Perry Preschool study through age 40.* Ypsilanti, MI: High/Scope.

Jones, R. (1991). *Matthew and Tilly.* New York: Trumpet.

Kingore, B. (2007). *Assessment: Timesaving procedures for busy teachers,* 4th ed. Austin, TX: Professional Associates Publishing.

Kingore, B. & Kingore, J. (2007). *Assessment Interactive CD-ROM.* Austin, TX: Professional Associates Publishing.

Leahy, S., Lyon, C., Thompson, M., Wiliam, D. (2005). *Classroom assessment: Minute by minute, day by day.* Educational Leadership 63(3), 19-24.

MacLachlan, P. (1985). *Sarah, Plain and Tall.* New York: HarperCollins.

Marzano, R. (2004). *Building background knowledge for academic achievement: Research on what works in schools.* Alexandria, VA: Association for Supervision and Curriculum Development.

Marzano, R. (2006). *Classroom assessment & grading that work.* Alexandria, VA: Association for Supervision and Curriculum Development.

Marzano, R., Pickering, D., & Pollock, J. (2001). *Classroom instruction that works: Research-based strategies for increasing student achievement.* Alexandria, VA: Association for Supervision and Curriculum Development.

McGuire, R. (1994). *Night becomes day.* New York: Viking.

McTighe, J. & O'Connor, K. (2005). *Seven practices for effective learning.* Educational Leadership, 63 (3), 10-17.

National Association for the Education of Young Children & National Association of Early Childhood Specialists in State Departments of Education. (2003). *Early childhood curriculum, assessment, and program evaluation: Building an effective, accountable system in programs for children birth through age 8. Position statement.* Washington, DC: Author.

National Reading Panel (NRP). (2000). *Teaching children to read: An evidence-based assessment of the scientific research literature on reading and its implications for reading instruction.* Jessup, MD: National Institute for Literacy at ED Pubs.

Numeroff, L. (2002). *If you take a mouse to school.* New York: Laura Geringer Books, HarperCollins.

Pittelman, S., Heimlich, J.E., Berglund, R.L., & French, M.P. (1991). *Semantic feature analysis.* Newark, Delaware: International Reading Association.

Sachar, L. (1998). *Holes.* New York: Farrar, Straus, & Giroux.

Shepard, L. (1997). *Measuring achievement: What does it mean to test for robust understanding?* Princeton, NJ: Educational Testing Service.

Smith, D. (2007). *If the world were a village: A book about the world's people.* Toronto, ON: Kids Can Press.

Sousa, D. (2001). *How the brain learns,* 2nd ed. Thousand Oaks, CA: Corwin Press.

Stronge, J. (2002). *Qualities of effective teachers.* Alexandria, VA: Association for Supervision and Curriculum Development.

Sylwester, R. (2003). *A biological brain in a cultural classroom,* 2nd ed. Thousand Oaks, CA: Corwin Press.

Tomlinson, C. (2003). *Fulfilling the promise of the differentiated classroom.* Alexandria, VA: Association for Supervision and Curriculum Development.

Vygotsky, L. (1962). *Thought and language.* Cambridge: MIT Press.

Walton, R. (2006). *Around the house the fox chased the mouse: A prepositional tale.* Salt Lake City, Utah: Gibbs Smith.

Wiggins, G. & McTighe, J. (2005). *Understanding by design,* 2nd ed. Alexandria, VA: Association for Supervision and Curriculum Development.

Willis, J. (2006). *Research-based strategies to ignite student learning: Insights from a neurologist and classroom teacher.* Alexandria, VA: Association for Supervision and Curriculum Development.

Willis, J. (2007). *Brain-friendly strategies for the inclusion classroom.* Alexandria, VA: Association for Supervision and Curriculum Development.

Willis, J. (2007). The neuroscience of joyful education. *Engaging the Whole Child,* 64, Summer.

Wolfe, P. (2001). *Brain matters: Translating research into classroom practice.* Alexandria, VA: Association for Supervision and Curriculum Development.

Young, E. (1992). *Seven blind mice.* New York: Scholastic.

Current Publications by
Bertie Kingore, Ph.D.

VISIT DR. KINGORE ONLINE!
www.BertieKingore.com

FOR INFORMATION OR ORDERS CONTACT:
PROFESSIONAL ASSOCIATES PUBLISHING
PO Box 28056 • Austin, Texas 78755-8056
Toll free phone/fax: 866-335-1460
E-mail: info@kingore.com

VISIT US ONLINE!
www.kingore.com

The rubrics in this book were created using:

Assessment Interactive CD-ROM

Bertie Kingore & Jeffery Kingore
Grades: K - 12

NEW!

This fully interactive and customizable CD-ROM provides the forms from the *Assessment* book, almost all of which are **completely customizable**. If computers are available in the classroom, students can also complete the assessments on the computer to save and print! Included are:

- Tier I, II, and III of the Rubric Generator.
  - An expanded pictorial rubric generator to use to build rubrics as posters or handouts for young learners or ELL students,
  - An expanded rubric generator with two tiers to choose from dozens of customizable criteria or to develop your own, creating an endless number of rubrics on the computer in minutes, and
- Over 140 completely customizable self-evaluations, assessments, interviews, conference forms, goal-setting forms, product grids, learning options posters, borders, and parent letters!

Professional Associates Publishing

PO Box 28056 • Austin, Texas 78755-8056
Toll free phone/fax: **866-335-1460**
www.kingore.com